800 Meters

A Journey of Addiction, Recovery and Redemption

Mikael Luman

Generation Free Press

For further information, please contact:
www.800meters.com

Printed in the United States of America

800 Meters: A Journey of Addiction, Recovery and Redemption
Mikael Luman

1. Title 2. Author 3. Self-Improvement/Addiction & Recovery

LCCN: 2007904584   .

ISBN-10: 0-9797374-0-0
ISBN-13: 978-0-9797374-0-4

*I dedicate this book to my daughter Mikaila,
my son Pearce, and my wife Amanda. I love you.*

TABLE OF CONTENTS

ACKNOWLEDGEMENTS

While writing this book I have often asked myself, *Why me?*

I have come to the conclusion that physical pain is nothing compared to the emotional pain of not doing all that I can to make a difference.

I'd like to give a special thank you to my daughter, Mikaila, whose birth inspired me to pursue my calling and focus on my foundation.

I'd also like to thank: My son Pearce—on his seventh birthday I began training for my 12,000-mile bicycle trip.

My wife Amanda—without your love and support, this book wouldn't have been possible. I love you.

My biggest fans—my parents, David and Patricia—without your forgiveness, consistent cheering and love, I wouldn't be here today.

Marianne—our relationship and friendship has come along way. Thank you for being the best mom possible to Pearce.

Bonnie Hearn Hill, for the editorial input and encouragement.

My high school coach, Ken Yarnell—thank you for believing in me then and now.

To all my high school friends, you know who you are: Thank you for all the memories both past and present. I am honored to still be able to call you friends.

To Bobby J—I will always strive to "keep it under 90." You inspire me more than you know.

To anyone I may have hurt, offended, lied to, stolen from or deceived, I sincerely apologize.

To all of the addicts and recovering addicts— I pray that you too will find your path.

INTRODUCTION
HOW DID THIS HAPPEN TO ME?

On Friday, October 20, 2000 at approximately 2053 hours, members of the Columbia Enforcement Narcotics Team (CENT) with the assistance of the Columbia County police department and the Oregon State police executed a search warrant at 50291 Columbia River Hwy in Scappoose, Oregon for a suspected methamphetamine lab. The search revealed an active methamphetamine lab in operation, along with a large amount of controlled substance methamphetamine that was in both marketable form and in solution. I led the team members to the rear entry door of the residence. I knocked on the rear door and three (3) times very loud announced 'Police! Search Warrant!' After I knocked for the third time, I forced open the door with a (key) ramming tool.

—Police report

Scappoose, Oregon. October 20, 2000. I was getting high after manufacturing a batch of meth when I saw the lights outside the patio door. Then someone pounded on the back door and shouted, "Police! Search warrant!"

Running from the cops was usually fun for me. I liked the rush. Besides, I always thought I could get away because I was an athlete. But this time I was scared—because I was tired, because I'd been on the run too long—and because I didn't think I was going to get away again. "Police! Search warrant!" usually means the house is surrounded. I went through the front door with my shoulder down expecting to knock through somebody. Miraculously, no one was out there. I bounced off the porch and across the wet grass. Then I leapt over the fence and ran for my life. *This is it*, I thought. *I'm done. The dogs and police must be right behind me.*

Running was part of my life then, not just from police but from problems. I always slept with my shoes on, just in case. When you're doing drugs and living the lifestyle the way I was, you're worried about getting locked up, but not worried enough to stop doing what you're doing.

Before, I would have just moved to another place, another town—I'd done it enough times. This time, I didn't. Maybe I was tired of running.

Could this be you? Have you assumed, as I did, that you can get away with anything just because it feels good at the start? For me it was the cockiness that came from my years as an athlete. I had the mindset, "Once an athlete, always an athlete." Despite the fact that I was now a drug addict, in my head I still saw myself as a track runner. Running from the cops just seemed like another race I was sure I could win. How wrong I was.

I'm not going to preach to you, but I would like to share what happened to me—a confident, good-looking star athlete, the guy who could talk his way out of anything and verbally tap dance around any issue and anyone who questioned him.

Much of what happened to me—both the ups and the downs—has to do with what I think of as my special calling. We all have a special calling, of course, but I was reminded of mine from as early as I can remember. My mother said that she saw me in my infant chair one day and just knew that I was different from her other children. She said a warm kind of feeling came over her that this child of hers was a special spirit. My grandmother had a similar vision. Once they shared their visions with me, those visions became my visions, and ultimately my burdens.

At first, I thought that calling had to do with my athletic abilities. As you will soon see, my early life revolved around those gifts. Still, I was never able to change my athletic expectations from sixth grade to high school or even after prison boot camp. I always tried to get by on natural ability alone, and I had lot of it. As I grew older, I could neither adapt my expectations nor change my habits. If I was at a practice, I gave it one hundred and ten percent. But if it was a weekend, and if I had more important things to do—or probably just more fun things to do—I usually lacked both the discipline and the desire to train. There's a difference between physical training and mental training. I think that I was born with the physical talent, but it was a long time before I started developing the mental capacity to cope with life's many struggles—which I am still working on today.

Looking back, I think I was an addict from the start. I was hooked before my first kiss, my first drink, my first bowl of weed, my first acid trip, my first tab, my first line of coke, my first pipe of crystal meth. There was a void in my life and I filled that void with sports. The less I was able to compete, the more there was to fill. Finally, it got to the point where I was filling it with partying, girls and drugs beyond anything I'd imagined. I was never very open with my feelings before I started to drink and use, because I didn't think anybody would understand. I think that ties into the sports. I was ADHD and I was obsessive compulsive, and the only times I felt really comfortable was if I was competing, acting out, hanging out with my friends or anything else to fill the void.

On the track

Track is not like team sports. Track is you alone. If something goes wrong, you don't have anyone to blame but yourself; the pressure is on you. There were two races that I ran during my track career that stood out from the others: the 800 meters and the 400 meters. The 800 meters is a mental race. You have to think, pace, learn and plan. You can't be all on or all off. Then there's the 400 meters. You just go out and run as fast as you can from start to finish—just sprinting when you hear the sound of the gun.

I lived my life the way I ran the 400. I was only looking toward the finish line and trying to get there the fastest way possible. I was always able to talk or lie my way out of almost any problem I brought on myself. If all else failed, my parents would help bail me out. I didn't learn until recently that I should have been running the 800 from the get go.

I didn't go from being perfect to using drugs, and I don't think people in general do that. I think it's a process. The more bad things you do, the less effect the good things have. The more depressed you get, the worse you feel, and the easier it is to make poor choices. This book will show you the decisions that led to my arrests, to prison and to my rehabilitation and redemption. At the time, many of them seemed like the wrong decisions, but now I'm not so sure that decisions can be right or wrong.

I believe that good decisions and bad decisions are ultimately judged by what you learn from them. At the time, a bad decision might feel wrong, but the ultimate outcome may be good. We're all potential winners; it just depends on our choices. These are the choices I needed to make to get where I am today.

Maybe you think your life could never get out of control. Perhaps you think that you are too strong to let addictions rule your choices. That's what I thought too. After all, I had a special calling.

Writing this book has been both a painful and a cleansing experience for me. It's important that you know before we continue that all of the people I write about in the following pages are real, although of course, their names have been changed. I didn't invent them. I didn't combine them. There are no composites or fictional characters, and all of the events and conversations are as accurate as I can recall.

CHAPTER ONE

RACING FOR MY LIFE

Mikael is training to be an Air Force pilot and to be running in the Olympics. Before he dies he wants to have run the Boston Marathon and to be in the Iron Man Triathlon in Hawaii.
—Mikael Luman,
written for a homeroom assignment in seventh grade

I wish someone had told me at an early age that perfection is never attainable. But then again, even if they had, I probably wouldn't have listened. I was always competitive in every aspect of my life. My house was about two miles from the school, and from the time I was in the first or second grade, I would ride my bike to the bus stop at the bottom of this little hill and wait with the other kids, including a cute girl named Emily, who was probably a good part of the reason I did it. I had no intention of getting on the bus; I was there to race. When I spotted the bus at the top of the hill, I took off riding. Right before we got to school, there was another hill, and it was always just the bus and me racing up the hill. I never lost.

I can remember running the mile in sixth grade, just two other guys and me—all of us close to winning. The possibility of losing overcame me; it was unbearable.

"Why don't we just tie?" I asked. They slowed down; I bounded ahead. I couldn't help it. Back then, betraying my friends didn't feel that bad. I wasn't running to win. I was running so that I wouldn't lose.

In sixth grade and ninth grade, I got the most outstanding male athlete award. I felt that athletics would be the map for my future, that I could travel as far as I wanted to, But a part of me also knew that I wasn't following any map but my own, because my path contained way too many shortcuts.

Two sides

I was the least likely candidate to end up on drugs. I grew up in a Christian family, we attended church every Sunday.

In elementary school, I was in a Safety Kids skit and I was one of the main characters. The message was about believing in yourself and not using drugs. The father of one of our good friends was a dentist who had been addicted to cocaine. He came to school and talked to us in seventh or eighth grade about how his addiction ruined his life. I was always taught that we shouldn't drink and that we should say no to drugs. But when you're so sheltered from addiction, you've got that distance, so you're never saying *no* to its face; you don't really know what you're saying *no* to because you've never seen it.

In one of the photo albums my mom has, there's a picture of me sleeping. Beside it, my mom wrote: "The only time Mikael was quiet was when he was asleep." Mom was right. I was always either talking or engaged in some activity. I was never able to just sit still and think. No matter what was going on inside my head, I always appeared happy and smiling.

There were two different sides to me back then. On the outside, it appeared that my life was easy and I had everything, but it wasn't as easy as it appeared. No one was aware of how much I struggled with perfectionism or the difficulty I had getting in touch with my emotions or expressing my feelings. People used to say, "Why are you always so happy?" They couldn't see the other me.

My paternal grandparents lived about ten minutes away. I spent a lot time helping my grandmother, who was in a wheelchair, with gardening, housework and shopping. Even when I was eighteen, nineteen and twenty, she'd still call to say she needed me to come over, and I'd go. She taught me a great deal, including how to do crewel embroidery and needlepoint. I still have a couple of pieces that I completed, including one that, for some reason, I did when I was on drugs. Needlepoint took longer for me than for most people because if there were ever any stitches even the slightest bit off, I would take them out and redo them. I was the same way building model airplanes, boats or cars.

Even after I was using, I was a perfectionist. When you're addicted to drugs, you're not at work by eight in the morning. It's hit or miss at best. Yet a woman whose house I painted told me one day when I was late, "I don't care if you show up at ten. I don't care if you show up at noon. I know that when the job is done, it's going to be perfect." I didn't care how long it took me. I just wanted to be sure it was right.

How I grew up—and down

In a way, I was a fearless kid, because I'd never experienced anything to make me otherwise. When my friend and I were in sixth grade, we found a hollow point bullet on top of a table in my dad's shop. I thought the hollow tip meant it had already gone off. We got pliers and a hammer, and as I was trying to pry the bullet apart, it exploded. We were in a confined area, and the sound was deafening. I covered my ears because they were ringing, and suddenly realized that blood was running down my face. At first I didn't know where it was coming from. Then we realized it was my hand, where a piece of the casing was stuck. I had to go to the hospital and have microsurgery to repair the nerves.

Although I was fearless for myself, I was worried for other people. Workers were doing construction on the houses down the street. After they'd gone home, I would walk on the top of the framed walls of one of the two-story houses with no problem, but when my little brother would get up there, I'd make him get down because I was afraid he was going to fall.

Growing up, I always wanted to help people, and I wanted them to like me. If the neighbors needed someone to babysit, I was there. I had a way with kids. I could just look in their eyes and know what they were thinking or feeling. For me, it reaffirmed that my special calling involved working with people.

Girls, girls, girls

I liked girls from an early age; it was always a game with me. I wanted all of the girls to like me, and I would do whatever it took—lie, cheat or steal—to get them to. It was just like running in P.E.—no rules.

The first girl I kissed was my outdoor school counselor. I was in sixth grade, and the counselors were in eleventh or twelfth grade. Everyone was giving me a hard time, saying the counselor had a crush on me. We spent a week at outdoor school, which was really like camping. The counselors from high school were there. One night after everyone was in bed, one of the male counselors came to the cabin and got permission for me to leave with him. I didn't have a clue about what was going on. I didn't know if I was in trouble or if there had been a family emergency. To my surprise, he brought me to meet the female counselor. We ended up kissing. It was a good thing I'd seen *Top Gun,* or else I wouldn't have had a clue how to pull that one off. Everyone thought it was this huge deal. For me it was the beginning of a new sport—kissing girls. I might not have been on top of my game that time, but I vowed to get better with practice.

Strange encounter of the first kind
Close to Cooper Mountain—our elementary school—was a field and an old barn. I was at the school with my dad and sister playing basketball. My friend James and his neighbor Blair were checking out a barn across the street. They said they'd heard there were boats in it. The run-down structure didn't look as if it would hold anything of value. My dad and sister stayed at the school, and we went to the barn. One of the windows was open, so we went inside and started walking around. There were some really nice boats inside that place. We couldn't figure out who'd put them there or why. The next thing I knew, a couple of guys were standing in there with us.

"You need to get out of here," one of them said.

My friend had a really scared look on his face. Then I saw why; one of them had a gun and was pointing it at us.

They were in their twenties, and I don't know if it was a real gun or a pellet gun, but it looked real to me. We climbed out the window and ran back to the school yelling and screaming. Once my dad saw what was going on, he climbed out of the Suburban, jumped over the fence and started chasing those guys. He never found them. After that, my friends and I were always talking about the boat barn and making up stories about why the boats might have been there, but we never went back. It was the first time I had a gun pulled on me, but not the last.

Looking back
At this age, most kids probably don't think about more than immediate gratification. Although I knew the difference between right and wrong, I didn't realize that poor decisions lead to more poor decisions. I tried to do right most of the time, but if doing wrong benefited me more at the moment, I didn't think about the long-term consequences. Perhaps if there had been some type of proactive education available when I was in grade school, I might have made different decisions.

CHAPTER TWO
HIGH SCHOOL TRACK

I wish I had known about your fear of losing at that point in your life so that I could have given you some ideas on how to deal with it in a positive way.
—Forrest Hall, grade school P.E. teacher

My athletic abilities were clear from the start. I climbed Mt. Hood twice when I was growing up—one of the most difficult runs in the area. I participated in the Hagg Lake Triathlon when I was fourteen and was the youngest one in the event. Also at the age of fourteen, I took part in the Hood to Coast Relay, a one-hundred-seventy-mile relay with twelve team members.

In the ninth grade in track, I won the 1,500- and 800-meter races at the district track meet. At this time in my career, I still had the confidence. I just went out there and ran, and I always won. The 1,500 is a three-and-three-quarter-lap race. The objective is to set a good pace early. You don't want to push the pace too hard, and you can't be too far ahead nor too far behind. You want to be sure everyone else is running your race. My strengths were my endurance, and I had a good kick. It's rare for a junior high student to participate in the high school district track meet, but the high school track coach, Ken Bell, said that if I ran a fast enough race, I would be able to.

I had pretty good speed going for a 1,500-meter race. I ran the first couple of laps fairly conservatively. On the start of the third lap, I began to push the pace a little bit. With three hundred yards to go, I started my kick early, left the pack behind and accelerated all the way to the finish line. I ran a 4:26, my fastest time by about seven seconds.

Running a double in a track meet means running two events. This is difficult because there are only about sixty minutes between each event. Most of the runners in the 800 were fresh; they hadn't run any other races. I was coming right from the 1,500. The 800 is a two-lap race. With one lap to go, I was in third place. Then a guy shot past me and took off. With three hundred yards to go, I was so tired that I didn't think I was going to win, and I tried to convince myself that it was okay because I'd won the other race. In my mind, I'd given up.

Then I heard someone on the sidelines say, "Oh, it looks like Mikael's going to lose."

Just hearing that was enough to change my mindset. I began to kick with everything I had left and closed the distance. Inches before the finish line, I passed the guy and won.

High school district track meet

When I climbed on the bus to go to the district high school meet a week later, I wore my usual green fluorescent jacket, which made me stand out from the rest of the competitors. The high school coach came up and told me I should take off my jacket and not be so cocky. He was probably preparing me to lose because I wasn't going to win against the high school kids. An older kid in the group taunted me and said, "There's no way you're going to beat me." That gave me motivation to try.

In that 1,500 race, I was competing against kids who were much faster. Instead of being able to push the pace, I was struggling just to keep up. There were two different heats, and I was in the slower one. With two hundred yards to go, the arrogant older kid who'd challenged me on the bus was ahead of me. I told myself that I could at least beat him. I did. My time was 4:19, and I placed third.

Prior to my sophomore year, I always won. It was a way of life for me. But competing against juniors and seniors, I didn't always win. People who didn't know me didn't expect me to win, but my parents, coaches and friends, who knew my abilities, wanted me to win. My personal record for the 800 was 200.3 seconds, and that was run a month before at an invitational meet we'd gone to.

In the district meet in the 800, I ran the prelims and was one of the eight to run in the finals. In the 800, I wanted to run my first lap in fifty-eight seconds and my second in sixty seconds. There was no way I thought I could win first or second though. We went out in about fifty-six seconds, so it was a pretty fast first lap. I thought it was way too fast, but with about two hundred fifty yards, I was able to snap myself into that zone the way I had in my freshman year. At that point, I could start my kick.

Coming down the straightaway, I saw somebody in front of me. It's easier when there's someone you're trying to catch. As I approached the finish line, he kind of leaned into me and knocked me over. When I put my hands down to catch my fall, I broke my middle finger, but I didn't realize it at the time. I was thrilled that I'd run the race in 157.7 seconds. My coach came to congratulate me, and when he took my hand, the pain was excruciating. My finger was lying sideways, and I still had the mile relay to run.

My dad, who thought my finger was dislocated, said to just tape it up, but the coaches wouldn't let me run. It was a spiral fracture, and it took three pins to keep it in place.

Although I didn't know it then, that moment of personal victory, fractured finger and all, was probably the climax of my sports career. Ken Bell, my track coach, was pretty excited and impressed. He wanted me to be a star as much as I wanted to be one. Still I knew this wasn't the fastest I could have run and wished I'd put out just a little more effort. Overall, though, I was happy. My times just kept getting better and better, and I was getting closer and closer to where I wanted to be. My next goal was the state championship and eventually the Olympics. Little did I know that this was the fastest I'd ever run the 800.

Looking back

Now I know if there's a goal that I want to attain, I have processes that I put into place to accomplish it. But not then. The type of athlete I wanted to be, the type of person I wanted to be, the type of son I wanted to be were only vague ideas. I had goals and dreams, but I never took action to make sure I achieved those goals or made those dreams come true.

CHAPTER THREE
FROM FIRST TO WORST

When I think of all the Warriors I've coached, you are the one I will always remember. Today, few three-sport athletes exist. Your ability to do this is a testament not only to your natural ability, but to your competitive spirit and great work ethic. Never lose these qualities as you strive to be your best self academically, professionally and personally.
—Coach Ken Yarnell

In my junior year, I played on the varsity basketball team, and we'd already had several preseason games. Our first regular season was against Tigard. With one minute left in the first quarter, I stole the ball and was going to lay it up. When I jumped, one of the players from the other team undercut me. When I came down, I landed right on my kneecap. It wasn't the first time I'd ever landed on my knees and although I knew it hurt like crazy, I continued to play through the pain.

At halftime, I went down and had the trainer look at my knee and wrap it up. Then I went out in the second half and started playing. My knee got stiffer and stiffer, and the pain increased. Finally, I had to come out of the game. Afterwards, in the locker room, the coach was giving us the customary talk. My leg was bent slightly, and I began to unwrap it. My kneecap area just blew up.

"Coach," I said, "there's something wrong."

My dad came down and took me to the hospital. In the emergency room, it was x-rayed and they told me I'd broken my kneecap, put a white plaster cast on it hip to foot and said that I needed to see a specialist. This was on Friday. On Monday, the specialist called and said that we should put screws in it. It didn't matter to me. All I was really concerned about was how long I'd be out.

I had the cast on for a month, and I wanted to play. When the doctor took off the cast, I asked him for a note clearing me to use the weight room. Once I had the note, I added a check to the list indicating that I was cleared for playing, too. My dad and I had a brace made, and with screws in my knee, I still played the last two games.

Up until this point, I was able to say *no* to drinking, but now I didn't care. My parents had gone out of town for the weekend, and James, J.D. and Aaron came over to the house to drink beer. The alcohol was there, and they were chugging it down. Watching them, I had that overwhelming, my-life-is-over feeling. It seemed that I had tried so hard to get to that point, and now look what had happened to me. I gave in and joined my friends in drinking beer. It numbed the pain of my disappointment and gave me false confidence, which at the moment was better than no confidence at all.

I was so disappointed that I couldn't look past the injury for a plan or solution to go on. As soon as I was able to start running, I should have been training. Instead, I was out drinking. The alcohol clouded my judgment and kind of took away what was important to me, moving me farther off center.

At the first race in that track season, I ran a 158.1 800 meter. At that point, I was happy, but I was also upset with myself that I hadn't trained more. A couple of meets later, I was to run against Seth Wetzel, another top athlete in the district. I was afraid to lose, afraid to run against him, afraid he was better than me. I'd experienced some pain in my knee up to that point, and all of that kept me from running a good race.

It was a cold, windy day, and I used pain as an excuse not to give the race my best. I finished third, and the *Oregonian* wrote:

> Wetzel expected to face some stiffer competition in the 800 from Mikael Luman of Aloha, who had the league's second-fastest returning time in the event behind Wetzel's electronically timed 1:52.94. But Luman faded in the rain and the wind and finished third behind Wetzel and Bert Passadore of Jesuit in 2:06.9.

My dad called the newspaper, and the next day, there was an article about how the screws in my knee slowed me down. Still, I don't think it was the knee. I think the problem was in my head.

I did make it to the state track meet in the mile relay, but again it was running the 400. Even though I wasn't able to run the 800 faster, my 400 was a second and a half faster than I'd run the year before. We placed third.

That summer I had surgery to remove the screws from my knee. I also had surgery on my hand to correct the finger I'd broken. In summer basketball, I broke my ankle, and I had a cast on that. I know that it sounds as if I had a lot of injuries. I don't think it's because I was accident-prone, however. I always gave it one hundred and ten percent. It was either all off or all on, and in those days, I was still on.

Senior year

In my senior year, Coach Bell always told me that considering how fast I ran the 400, I should not only be able to win the state 800 but possibly break the state record. I was able to run a second faster in the 400, but I was never able to run the 800 as fast as I had my sophomore year.

It was the district track meet. My whole career was riding on this race. If I placed first or second, I would go to the state championship meet. When the race started, we went out in fifty-five seconds the first lap. With three hundred meters to go, I was still in first place. Maybe the pressure got to me. I don't know. The next thing I remember was walking across the finish line in last place. I thought my whole life was over. That was it. I was in shock.

In the mile relay, I was so mentally unprepared that I grabbed the baton, cut to the inside to go around three people and took too many steps on the white line. I didn't realize until after the race was over that I'd gotten the team disqualified. We finished third, not the first or second we needed to go to the state championship meet.

Recently I found the baton from that race—broken. I'd snapped it in half after the race when we were going back on the bus. The broken baton reminds me of the anger and frustration I felt at not living up to my expectations for myself. However, upon graduating, I still received the most outstanding athlete award from the US Navy. With all of my injuries, I was still probably the best athlete in the school. But I wasn't the best athlete I could have been. I never ran another track race.

Looking back

There's a difference between training for something and participating in it. When something out of one's control occurs, there are two different types of responses: coming back stronger or not coming back at all. Instead of using my injury as a positive, developing a plan and coming back stronger, I used it as an excuse and a justification to do whatever I wanted.

CHAPTER FOUR
NO CONSEQUENCES

*Growing up, Mikael was always the squeaky clean guy of the bunch.
He was always the one you depended upon, always the guy who was
the designated driver or the one you could call on
when you needed help.*
—Aaron, a high school friend

It took me a long time to learn that there are consequences for every action, because for a long time, I got away with everything I did. My dad frequently did my homework and wrote my term papers. He also wrote notes saying I had a doctor's appointment when I'd really slept in. He gave me his 1982 Suburban when I was sixteen. Black with chrome wheels, it had four inches of lift and thirty-five-inch tires. My friends loved it, and we took it everywhere. That truck gave us power. Most of all, it gave *me* power.

That year, I was racing one of my friends, who was stopped in the left-hand turn lane. I continued to go straight, and at the last minute on a red light, I cut back across traffic. I didn't think about what would happen if I got pulled over.

After I had stopped and parked on the sidewalk to wait for my buddy, one of my parents' friends pulled up to me, told me I was an idiot and said he was going to call my folks. *Go ahead and do it*, I thought. I wasn't worried. I always did whatever I wanted, never caring about the repercussions, because there never were any that I couldn't get out of or at least deal with. Besides my parents still believed that everything I told them was the truth.

That attitude led to my hitting cars on purpose when someone crossed me. It happened on more than one occasion, for the first time when I was sixteen. James, Aaron and I were cruising Broadway, the main drag, in my Suburban, looking for girls. A car kept stopping in front of us, preventing us from talking to the girls who were next to them. When I finally pulled up beside the car, I said, "If you stop in front of me again, I'm going to hit you."

Twenty minutes later, we were stuck in the same situation. He stopped in front of me opposite those girls we wanted to talk to. When I got close enough, I stuck my head out the window and said, "You stopped in front of me again. I told you I'd hit you if you did."

The guy yelled back, "You won't hit me."

I turned the wheel and stepped on the gas. After I smashed the side of his car with the Suburban's big metal bumper, I drove off.

He tried to chase us down, but I was too skilled a driver and got away.

A couple of weeks later, we were downtown again on a side street, and there was not a lot of traffic. A car stopped in front of me, and a bunch of guys jumped out. I rolled up my window. One of them was the same guy I'd hit weeks before. They started yelling at us to get out of the car, threatening to kick our butts.

I calmly opened the sun roof, stood up and said to the driver, "You'd better move your car, or I'm going to hit it."

This time, he believed me and they left us alone.

Everybody always wanted to sit shotgun in my truck. James was my best friend, so he usually got the prized seat. One time when we were going to Seaside on spring break during our senior year, Steve and James got into an argument about who was going to sit shotgun.

So I threw them the boxing gloves I always kept in the truck and said, "Hey, why don't you guys box for it?" James was this two-hundred-pound guy who never worked out a day in his life and didn't need to. Steve was the athletic, bike-riding type guy—not too much muscle. But, Steve said, "Okay, I'll fight you for it."

James boxed like a pro, and Steve wasn't getting any punches in. Then he just threw a huge hit out of nowhere, and it landed on James' chin and knocked him out. So Steve got to sit shotgun that trip.

Seaside was one of our favorite destinations for spring break. About a seventy-minute trip from Beaverton, it was a small town, but packed with kids that time of year. We developed some pretty innovative pick-up lines. One was taking a golf ball and tossing it into a group of girls. Then, we'd walk right into the group saying, "Excuse me, excuse me," and kind of elbow our way in.

Someone would always ask, "What do you think you're doing?"

And I'd reply, "Excuse me. We're just playing through. I've got to take a shot."

That of course led to conversation, and pretty soon we were with the girls.

I was never a fighter, and the senior trip to Seaside stands out as the only time in school I ever got beat up. We started drinking right away. I'd had two forty-ouncers, and I was pretty drunk.

There was a small strip with people walking all over the place, partying. I looked up and saw this good-looking girl coming toward me. As she was walking by, I reached out for her hand. Only one problem: I didn't realize that her hand was attached to someone else's. Next thing I knew, I was punched out and lying in the middle of the street.

I stood up and said, "What happened? Who hit me?"

The guy wanted more, and the crowd was wild. So now we were all going to head for the beach so that I could fight this guy. I was drunk enough to think that I could do it. More than that, I thought my friends would cover for me. Yet, when we got to the beach, none of my friends were there. *Where were all of these guys who were supposed to have my back?* I wondered.

I moved through a crowd of people and saw the guy. He was already taking his shirt off. There was no James, no Aaron. There was no anybody to help me. So it was like *wham, wham* into my face. I couldn't begin to hit back. I could barely see.

After I took three or four shots to the head, I got down in the fetal position, my hands over my face. The guy then proceeded to kick me a couple of times. I was drunk, beat up and lying there in pain. Then James arrived, realized what had happened and was calling the guy out, wanting to take on anyone and everyone.

Bottom line, I'd had my butt kicked for grabbing the hand of the wrong girl. But once that beautiful girl saw me beaten up, she actually felt sorry for me, and was angry with the guy for hurting me. We spent the night in my sleeping bag on the beach, and I felt better about my injuries.

The next day we were driving the strip, going to the Shiloh Inn to take a shower, which was one of our favorite tricks. Since we usually camped out for three or four days, we needed to find a free shower, and the hotel was it. The way we managed it was to sneak in after the people who'd rented a room left it to check out and before the cleaning people came in.

The Shiloh Inn was three stories tall, and the room we sneaked into was located on the third floor.

"I have to pee," James announced.

But someone was in the bathroom, and the door was locked. That didn't stop James. He stood inside the door and urinated off the balcony, over a two-lane street, and onto the other sidewalk. He was known for feats like this when we were partying. I thought it was impressive when he did that over the hood of my lifted Blazer, but this shocked even me.

I had no idea how fast time would move and how soon these Seaside summers would be only memories.

Double your money

When I was a junior in high school, James' neighbor, Blair, asked us if we'd like to invest in cocaine. We had no idea what cocaine was or what it did to you, but Blair said we could double our money. We couldn't even conceive of that. But we made our four-hundred-dollar investment (James' money, I must confess) and were already thinking of ways to spend the thousands of dollars we were going to make. It never happened. Blair ripped us off, and I had my introduction to the world of dealing.

You'd think that I learned my lesson, but the call of "double your money" would follow me for many years.

About the same time, five or six of us were going into a convenience store, around eleven-thirty at night, when a guy stopped us and asked if we'd like to buy some marijuana.

"Hey, if you guys have two hundred dollars, I can go up the street and get you an ounce of weed. You can go sell that ounce for three-twenty."

We all put in forty bucks, and we figured we'd be able to pay for the ski trip we'd just been on. The guy needed a ride up the street to get the weed, so we drove him in my truck and dropped him off in a rural area. And waited. We sat there for an hour and a half before I realized that he wasn't coming back.

I grew up around people who did what they said and who told the truth. Thus, I was completely unprepared for the world of drugs, where everybody lied.

Boxers and beer

In my senior year, I started stealing. I had a friend, Kent, who was into stealing boxer shorts. Don't ask me why. He just liked having lots of boxers. I went with him to the local Meier & Frank. The feeling I had when I took the boxers was amazement at how easy it was. I felt a rush and knew that I'd do it again.

My first brush with the law came on one of those days I'd shoplifted boxer shorts. We were spotted by an employee, followed and pulled over. I went to court and had to do community service but managed to keep it from my folks. This is when the criminal voice in my brain said, "Next time, do it differently." Not, "You shouldn't steal." Just, "Do it so you don't get caught."

The high of stealing was matched by the high of drinking, and doing both together was the best high of all back then. I was probably the last of my friends to drink. From the time I was about fifteen, I would drive them around when they got drunk. I started drinking about the middle of my sophomore year, and because I didn't yet have a fake ID—and because I liked the rush—I began stealing alcohol.

We'd go to a store, grab a couple of six-packs and head out again. We were planning a huge Fourth of July party, and I was in charge of the alcohol. I knew I couldn't keep running into the store for a couple of six-packs. My friend Kent worked at Safeway and he said, "Just come in, bag them up and push them out the door."

If you don't look like you're doing something wrong, you're not doing something wrong in the eyes of the public. The reason I was such a good thief is that I never thought that I was doing something wrong, so I didn't look it. It was just another game. I went in with empty bags, stuffed them with beer and then just rolled the cart out of the store.

One day, while stealing wine with my friend Aaron, I was spotted by a girl who'd attended high school with me—although I didn't know that until later. The store employees chased us, and someone else got in a car and came after us. Aaron dropped his wine and cut his hand on the broken glass, but we got away. The police left a citation at my house. Although the charges were dropped, my parents found out about that one, and so did Aaron's parents. They were upset with my parents and me because I was the one who had initiated it.

In my junior and senior years, my friends and I stayed at my parents' house most of the time. My friend James would often stay with us because he had issues with his dad, and it was just easier to hang out at my house.

We had a ritual after a night out drinking. We'd always stop down the street before we got home, and we'd make ourselves puke. Sometimes, we'd do it to ourselves, and if we were too drunk, we'd do it for each other. Gross, I know, but that's what we did. We were finished drinking, and the reason for drinking was to get drunk, right? We didn't want the alcohol to sit in our stomach all night. After you do twelve cans of beer in a beer bong, you sometimes have no other choice.

The night of our senior party, my three friends and I had three bottles of wine. We used a beer bong—that is a valve connected to the bottom of a tube. The trick was to have someone hold it, then drop down to your knees and open that thing up. Instead of beer that night, we beer-bonged the wine, which meant we each consumed a bottle within seconds. Then we went on the bus to our senior party. Ours was an all-nighter held at an athletic club. It started at ten p.m. and got over around six in the morning. My mom gave me a surprised look and said, "Your breath smells like alcohol."

"I just drank some juice," I said. "It must have been fermented."

Did she believe me? Parents want to believe their kids. They don't want to think that their kids are lying to them. They justify it in their minds just as much as the people lying to them justify it in their minds.

A lot of my drinking and drug use had to do with sports and not being able to compete. It filled the void and became my sport. Right at the end of high school, I tried marijuana for the first time. When I was about seventeen, I was driving with friends when they decided to do some.

"I'd never do that marijuana stuff," I said.

My friends broke up laughing, and one of them said, "You did marijuana last weekend."

"I did not," I insisted. "I smoked pot."

That's how naïve I was. I didn't even know the jargon.

As I said before, I think breaking my kneecap in my junior year damaged more than my body. Sports had been the one way I could let out the emotions I couldn't release any other way. With the summer between graduation and college ahead, I was no longer the athlete I'd dreamed of being. My dreams of an athletic scholarship had died, and I had no idea of what lay ahead.

Looking back

Life isn't over unless you're dead, but you couldn't have told me that back then. When I was injured, I went into a depression and started drinking. I didn't have a contingency plan. Little in life ever goes the way we expect it to. The successful people are the ones who are able to adapt and grow from adversity. I know now that when you set goals, you also have to have other plans in place in case something goes wrong.

CHAPTER FIVE
THE LAST SUMMER

Mikael's potential as a distance runner is unlimited. He possesses the speed, the work habits and the mental toughness to succeed at the Division 1 level. I feel that Mikael will do nothing but improve at the next level. He has both the ability and the desire to succeed.
—Coach Ken Bell in a letter to the track and field coordinator of Boise State University

Track season ended the end of May. Graduation was in June. From that period after track season, I have no idea how I managed to get through graduation. It's a good thing it was the last couple of weeks of my senior year where less was expected of me, because I was pretty much out of control. Drinking became not just a weekend thing. I was drinking and going to school. I was goofing around. I didn't even know where I was going to go to college until late June or early July.

From eight to twelve years old, like other boys in my church, I planned to go on a mission when I was nineteen. Some athletes attend Brigham Young University for one year, go on a mission and come back. In my sophomore year, my focus was obviously sports, so my mission plans kind of went out the window.

I'd always thought I was going to go to a four-year college and play sports, but in my junior and senior year when the recruiting was being done, my heart just wasn't in it because of my injury. I loved going to school because of sports and because I loved being around people. I would go to school and not even go to class just so I could hang out in the student lounge. For me, it was about the people, the girls, and of course, the attention.

After the district track meet when I'd finished last, my track coach, Ken Bell, who had recognized and nourished my potential, was so disappointed that he didn't talk to me for a while. Still he contacted the coach at Portland State, and he drove me down there to meet with him. The track coach said that I could run track there and about a week later, the soccer coach called and asked me to be on the soccer team. Practice would start in August, he said, a few weeks before school began.

Like a virgin

Maybe you think someone who'd done everything else I had in high school was having sex with every girl in town. The truth is that I was doing everything but. I'd already decided that I was not going to have sex before marriage. It was the last part of my belief system that I'd been able to hang onto. I knew that my friends were all doing it, but they didn't talk about it in front of me, and that was fine. I had plenty of action, but I wasn't going beyond my own boundaries. At least, that was what I told myself.

One night, my friend, Kent, his girlfriend, Kaylee, and I were partying with girls from Sunset High. We always liked to party with girls from different schools because we'd already gotten action from the girls at Aloha, and now they were more like friends. On that night we ended up on Sauvie's Island on Reeder Beach, and Stacy joined us. She was a beautiful blonde who I'd always noticed when we were out partying from the time we were sophomores, but she had a longtime boyfriend, and I didn't stand a chance with her.

However, they'd broken up just at the end of high school. I started talking to her that night, and she said, "I remember you from the first time I saw you driving around in your Suburban, and I've had a crush on you ever since."

This was the best-looking girl from Sunset High School. I couldn't believe my luck.

"I've had a crush on you too," I told her, which wasn't a lie. I had a crush on all the girls.

We started talking, kissing and fooling around. Up until that point, I'd always been more on the defensive when making out with girls. There was a certain point where I would back off. I'd do all of the touching because I wanted to stay in control. I didn't dare let the girl be in control, because I knew where it would lead. But this night was different. I was really drunk, and Stacy was experienced and aggressive. She knew what she wanted and told me what to do. I ended up going farther than I ever had with a girl, and I liked it.

The next night I went out with Kent and Kaylee and Stacy. I'd stolen some wine, and we went to the Columbia River gorge, hiked up to one of the waterfalls and got drunk. Kaylee and Kent were on one end of the bridge, and Stacy and I were on the other. Before I knew it, we were having sex.

Still unable to believe what had just happened, I went to the other end of the bridge and announced to Kent. "Hey, Kent, I just had sex."

"Well," he said. "Go back there and do it again."

Oh, I thought. I didn't even know that was an option.

After that, I was into it. I called every girl I'd turned down in the past to announce that I was having sex now. One actually took me up on it and offered to teach me.

A few days later Stacy and I went boating with some other friends. She'd just finished waterskiing and was still in the water beside the boat. Then somehow—probably the alcohol—I inadvertently called her by another girl's name, and she stopped speaking to me on the spot. She was the first girl I'd crossed my own boundary with, and she wouldn't even talk to me. When I saw her a couple of years later at a mall, I wasn't remotely attracted to her. But she was the first, like it or not. And with her, I'd broken the final rule that connected me to my faith and my teachings.

Going our separate ways

The second time I smoked marijuana was right before James left to go to California. Someone had given us a bud, and it was the first time I really felt the high. The first time we smoked it we'd gone to a laser light show, and I'd just kind of sat there and watched it. This time we were up in the woods in my truck, waiting for some other people to show up for a party. We made a pipe out of a can, and we started to sing to the tune of the children's song, "There's a hole in the bucket, dear Liza, dear Liza."

"There's a bud in my pocket, dear James, dear James. There's a bud in my pocket, dear James, some bud." He would answer, "Then smoke it, dear Mikael, dear Mikael." This went on for a while as we continued to add lyrics to our tune. I was feeling great.

The people showed up, and we partied up in the woods. When we left, we were driving up a hill in my Blazer. I knew what it sounded like when I broke a driveline. That's what I thought had happened. *Oh, no,* I thought. *The truck won't move. We're stuck at the bottom of this hill.* We were just sitting there; we didn't know what to do. And then, I came to find out, the drive line wasn't broken. The truck was fine. It was all in my mind. It was a half hour or forty-five minutes before we even realized that I should try to drive it.

James moved to California, where his mother lived; he was the first of my friends to leave town. That summer, Aaron and I drove to San Jose to visit him. This was the last time that Aaron, James and I partied together.

The phone sex guy

Aaron was getting ready to move, and Kent and James had already left for college. I missed my friends and knew that our lives were heading in different directions. Soccer season was arriving, so I went down to the practice. The first day we did a bunch of running so the coach could see what kind of shape we were in. After practice, I was talking to a guy named Alex, who had played soccer in California.

He was tall, almost seven feet, with dark hair, bleached at the tips. A preppy dresser, he had a wide, Jack Nicholson grin, and although he wasn't the best-looking guy, the girls always found him attractive.

"So you went to Aloha," he said. "My girlfriend went there."

"What's her name?" I asked.

He told me, and I couldn't help grinning. There was a cute girl in my P.E. class who was constantly talking about her California boyfriend and how they had phone sex all of the time. Back then it was too much information for me. I didn't want to hear about her guy down in California. If she wanted to fool around, she ought to be fooling around with me, right?

What are the odds of hearing about some guy from another state having phone sex with a girl you know, and then actually meeting the guy?

"Oh," I said. "You're the phone sex guy."

That was the beginning of us hanging out together. Alex asked where I lived, and when I told him Beaverton, he asked if I'd give him a ride home from practice. As it turned out, he lived in the apartments behind the Safeway where my friends and I had stolen alcohol. His roommates were in the process of moving out, and he needed a roommate. I'd been thinking about moving out of my parents' house. So we decided that I'd move in with him.

Alex and I picked our classes together. During the soccer season, I literally only went into the classroom two times. Both times we were laughing so hard about something stupid that we just got up and left class. It wasn't much of a beginning for my college career.

Tripping out

The first time I did acid was right before I moved in with Alex. I was hanging out with my other friend, Steve, the same one I smoked pot with the first time. He and his friends were kind of earthy types who were always riding their mountain bikes, and they been smoking pot and doing since they were about sixteen.

"Hey," he said. "We're going to do acid tonight. Do you want to do it?"

"I don't think so," I told him. "I have soccer practice in the morning, at eight."

"Oh, no problem. You'll be fine by then," he said.

The thing about drug people is that they always tell you whatever you want to hear at the time. They also tell you that scoring is going to be easier than it is—and earlier. If the drugs are supposed to arrive at nine, you can bet it will be closer to eleven, which is what happened to us that night. They also didn't mention to me how long the effects of acid would last.

We went downtown because we were supposed to meet the guys with the drugs down by OHSU—Oregon Health & Science University. It was eleven before we finally got it. We put the acid under our tongues and went to downtown Portland. There was a fountain down by the waterfront area and some benches overlooking the river. I was sitting on the bench, and they handed me these magnets to play with. So, I was sitting on the bench, pushing the magnets back and forth. When I finally looked up, buildings were different colors. The intensity of it was amazing.

They left me there for a long time. Then a truck pulled up, and these people said something I couldn't understand. I thought I knew them, and I ran after them down the sidewalk. I got all the way down to almost where the waterfront ends, and I couldn't see the pickup anymore. Totally confused, I started walking back up the waterfront. It was about two-thirty or three in the morning, and quiet. I could hear my friends' voices echoing through the building, and we managed to find each other. Coming through the tunnel from Portland to Beaverton, the lights of the cars were like a video game.

I dropped the others off, and Steve and I were still parked in the truck when I saw a police car in the school parking lot. Afraid to drive, I just sat there until almost five-thirty. I finally got out of the truck and walked over to the parking lot, and there wasn't even a car in there. I must have hallucinated it.

Finally, I got home. My mom was upset about the time, but I couldn't handle trying to deal with her. When I was drinking, I'd come home drunk and talk to her for an hour or more and not even remember it. On acid, I didn't even want to look at her. I'd just wanted to go to sleep. I lay on my bed, wide awake, tripping, wondering why I couldn't go to sleep.

I was still tripping out when I went to soccer practice. By the time practice was over, I was finally able to sleep.

When I told Alex about it the next day, he was shocked and couldn't believe what I had done. Two years later, when he'd dropped acid for the first time, he'd been instantly hooked. After that, I was a little bit afraid of acid. It was pretty intense, and I didn't like not being able to control the effects. Still, I continued to use it.

Bachelor pad

When Alex and I met, he was all about having sex with girls, and I was in competition with him. Then he got a girlfriend and that slowed him down. I didn't slow down. With me, it was always all or nothing.

As soon as soccer practice started, within two weeks, Alex's roommates had moved out, and I had moved into the two-bedroom apartment. Alex's first order of business was to get me a fake ID.

Back then, they didn't have pictures on file. I could go into the DMV and say I was anyone who was at least twenty-one. All I needed was their name, birth date, mother's maiden name and place of birth. I can still recite from memory today the information that I used. I would give them a checkbook and something else to verify the address, and I'd get a fake ID with my picture on it. I did that three different times.

When we'd originally started going to Lake Oswego Point, I'd get in line about eight or ten people ahead of Alex. After I gave them the fake ID, he would come in behind me. That didn't last long. We went to the club Thursday, Friday and Saturday; we were regulars. Soon we got to know the big guy at the door, and no one questioned my age or my identity. Not then, at least.

For me, going from a high school party at someone's house when their parents were out of town to a club like Lake Oswego Point was mind-boggling. There was a huge difference. If we didn't get there by seven p.m., the line was out the door and around the corner. It was my first experience with adult-type partying and as usual, I always overdid it.

Alex's roommates had taken the furniture with them. All we had was his bed and the new bed my parents bought for me. About that time, we met some soccer team buddies, Rod and Ethan, our goalkeeper. Rod was a professional nighttime thief. We started going out at night, when we came home drunk, we'd break into cars, steal wallets and checkbooks, that kind of stuff. When we were stealing to furnish our apartment, I started forging checks.

I bought a futon, a fish tank and other furnishings. At the same time, Ethan lived in upscale apartments his parents paid for. The complex was up above Portland, with a gated access road and entry. Each front door had a keypad and a camera.

At the time we were renting furniture from Peoples' Furniture. Now it was time to upgrade. When I was in the lobby one day, Alex and I looked at each other, and I knew that he was thinking as I was: that this was some pretty nice furniture out here in Ethan's lobby. The style back then was the black-and-white Ansel Adams look, and the leather couches and end tables would be perfect. I don't know what made me think *Hey, we should take them*, but we did say, "Hey, Ethan, you've got nice furniture in your lobby."

Our approach was to drive in there as if we were going to see Ethan, through the outside security, which was on the access road. Although all of the units had cameras on the front door, the side access didn't. But they were for exit only. That didn't stop me.

I climbed up outside and onto the first floor, and then I headed downstairs to let my friends in the side door so that we could sneak into the lobby and remove the furniture.

We did it three different times because we could put only so much in the truck. How stupid could we be? You rob somebody, and then you go back three times. Ethan didn't know we were doing it just yet, but someone should have known. That's how we got the bulk of our nice furniture—from Ethan's lobby.

Letting ourselves in
Alex had a key to an old apartment he used to live in at Country Fields. He went in there one day, but didn't take anything except a watch.

Alex said, "I wonder if the key still works."

"Let's go check it out," I said.

The key worked, and there was a bunch of really nice Ansel Adams framed photos. So we took the photos and went back into the bedroom, where I spotted four change cans. We grabbed them, we went out to the car, and when we started driving, I opened up one of them and found $1,500 cash in the top and about $500 in change.

The story came full circle, though. We were at Lake Oswego Point a few months later. By then, we'd become pretty good friends with the bar manager. He was about six foot seven, three hundred pounds—a big guy, bigger than James even. As we were talking, it came out that he lived at Country Fields.

Alex said, "Oh, I used to live at Country Fields. How do you like living there?"

He was wearing the infamous watch and immediately stuck his hand in his pocket because, from the look on the guy's face, we knew where the story was leading.

"I did like it," he said, "until this one day, I left for ten minutes to run down the street to the bank, and when I got back, someone had stolen my art and my money."

Damn, I thought. He'd been gone for ten, and we'd been in there for twelve minutes at least. This was one big guy. If he'd caught us, he would have ripped our heads off. What if he was playing a game with us, though? Did he know we were the ones who broke in?

"Did you ever find out who did it?" I asked, trying to look sincere.

"Well, yeah," he said. "A couple of days before that, my friend was over when I was gone, and the maintenance guy just happened to pop in. My friend was like what are you doing?" He was convinced it was the maintenance guy and got him fired from the apartment.

Alex and I looked at each other as if to say, "That was a close one."

The stealing continued, and Rod moved in with us. One night we came home drunk, and we were saying, "Gosh, the apartment sure has a nice audio system." So what did we do? We stole the audio/entertainment equipment out of our own apartment complex. It was two-thirty a.m. We were pushing a big screen on wheels and couldn't get it to fit in the back of my car, so we ended up leaving it on the corner so we could go back and get it.

The managers at the apartment kind of had a feeling that it was us, but they couldn't prove it. We partied at Lake Oswego Point with the people who worked at the complex. But I made the mistake of leaving a piece of the stereo equipment in my truck, and it would soon come back to haunt me.

Looking back

This was my point of no return. There was too much fun, too much partying, too many lies and too much underlying pain for me to be able to turn my life around. My sports life might have been over, but my partying life had just begun.

CHAPTER SIX
LIVING FOR TODAY

To summarize you in a word: fearless.
—J.D., longtime friend

Cocaine. I'd been warned about it all my life, but I had no idea how it would make me feel and how it would convince me it was satisfying the emptiness in my life. That's the problem with what well-meaning types tell you about drugs and alcohol. They say it's no fun. You try them and find out that it's fun as hell, and there you are, in the middle of a habit that can ruin your life. Drugs are fun at first, and so is alcohol. That's the truth. But the fun doesn't last long, take it from me.

Alex and I were at Lake Oswego Point one night when he went outside to do coke with a girl he had met there. She invited us over to her house to do some more. I was eighteen, and this was the first time I'd experimented with coke. I was bouncing off the walls, being silly and stupid. Driving home, I realized how much I liked the invincible feeling, that on-top-of-the-world feeling I'd soon experience with speed. I hadn't yet realized that the on-top-of-the-world feeling would soon become the driving force in my life.

Alex and I weren't as close as James, Aaron and I had been. But we clicked. We laughed at the same things and both had a sense of humor.

We were still playing soccer and not going to class—and drinking. Our drinking now took place before and after practice and all night.

Lake Oswego is not a very good place to be driving less than sober, especially in a truck like mine. We were driving in and out of there three nights a week, drunk. We'd wake up in the morning, and I'd ask, "What did we do last night? Who drove home?"

"Oh, you did, Mikael."

"I did? Well, how did I do?"

"You did pretty well."

Grand theft auto

One night we were leaving to go to the club when I noticed a Camaro next to my truck. We'd been drinking first, of course, because it was cheaper that way. We had a nice little arrangement going with one of the bartenders with whom we played poker. He wouldn't charge us for the drinks, but we would just tip him. We'd bring twenty dollars apiece. We'd also drink a little bit ahead of time so we had a little pre-funk going.

I looked at the Camaro and realized that it was running.

"That car's been running since we came home," I told Alex. "Well, that's really weird. Let's like maybe turn it off for the people."

The next thing you know, we're sitting in the car. Then, I'm stepping on the gas saying, "It feels like this car has quite a bit of power. Well, maybe we can find the people the car belongs to or something."

So, just like that, we drove to Lake Oswego Point in this stolen Camaro. We went, we partied and when we got back, we decided in all of our impaired wisdom that maybe we should park it down around the corner from our apartment. That was a Friday, and we didn't really want to give it back yet.

"Did we really steal that car last night?" I asked Alex the next morning. Before he could answer, I looked in my pocket and found the keys. "Yeah," I said, "we did."

It wasn't as if we just went for a joyride in the country. We stole a car and went to Lake Oswego Point. I'm still afraid of driving in Lake Oswego. It's a small town, the richest community in the area. The police pull you over for anything. Yet, three days a week, we drove right through the middle of it, just to go party, and the night before, we'd done it in a stolen Camaro.

When I first started engaging in criminal activities, all I could relate it to were TV experiences. In my head, I was thinking, *Oh, we'll get a storage unit and keep it forever. Or find a chop shop and sell it.* Well, number one, we didn't know where a chop shop was and two, we weren't going to pay to rent a storage unit to hide a car that wasn't even ours.

We drove the car a few other times. A week went by, and we got too drunk to remember to park it as far away as we had, so we just parked it where we'd first found it and went inside. The next morning it was moved somewhere else. I asked Alex, "What'd we do with the car?"

"We parked it where we found it," he said.

That day, there were signs posted all over our part of the complex. "Car thieves. We know who you are. Contact Washington County Sheriff's Department before they contact you." It wasn't just one sign but three or four different ones, but only right around where we lived.

Road trip

The good thing about college sports is that you get to travel. We were going up to Spokane and then to Canada for a weekend. Alex and I were sitting in the first row of the van, telling jokes and stories.

There was a guy on the team named C.J. All teams have a guy like this. He was the type who had all the gear—the watch, the shorts, socks and shoes—and little of the ability. He sucked at playing soccer, but if you looked at his gear, you'd think he was a good soccer player. On that day, he was showing off one those new Swatch watches with a removable band.

I said, "C.J., let me check out that watch."

He tossed it to me. I checked it out and threw it back to him.

C.J. couldn't play soccer, and he couldn't catch either. It was like in slow motion. I watched his hands, which looked like seal hands. I knew he wasn't going to catch the watch, but I hadn't counted on the window in the back of the van, which of course was open. The watch ricocheted off C.J.'s hand, off his vest, and then out the window. We were on the freeway going sixty-five. We weren't about to stop.

It was quiet. Everyone sensed that C.J.'s feelings were a little bit hurt. I didn't say anything for about five minutes, but then I couldn't hold it back any longer.

"Hey, C.J.," I said. "What time is it?" Everybody started busting up.

By the end of our trip, we were in Canada, and the coach said we had to be in our rooms by ten p.m. A couple of older guys said they were going to sneak out and go to the strip bar and invited me to go with them. I'd never been to a strip bar before, and I was pretty embarrassed. They made me sit in front, right up against the bar, and they tipped the girl to dance for me. I was blushing and embarrassed, but liked what I saw.

Breaking and entering

I couldn't keep getting away with what I was doing, and one night when I returned home from Lake Oswego drunk, my luck ran out. Across from our apartments were high-end apartments called The Lakes—which included furnished units. We were translating "furnished" into free TVs, VCRs and other electronics. Today, I'm not sure why this mattered to us. We'd already fully furnished our apartment with our stolen goods. Perhaps we planned to sell what we stole that night. Maybe we were just drunk and bored, and when we didn't come home with girls, we needed something to do.

I'd actually gone into The Lakes apartments a night or two before and asked them about their furnished units. Crazy, I know, but I looked pretty innocent, and I think they believed me. The manager walked me around the complex and showed me where the furnished units were; she even gave me a plot map.

That night, Rod and I parked up the street, kicked the door in and went inside. As soon as we did, I noticed there was a pair of shoes by the front door. We were both inside when we noticed the shoes, and we were both scared. In an instant, I realized that somebody must have lived there. It was only one or two days from the first time I'd gone through there, when it was vacant, but we knew that we needed to get out—and fast.

We got away, but not for long. Whoever was living there must have awakened and heard something, because they got a license plate number, which was registered to my dad.

The next thing I knew, my dad called and told me the police were looking for me. As Rod and I were leaving the apartment, the police were coming, so we ran. I shot down the end of the apartment complex, and I planned to go through the bushes and into the trees. I ended up diving into a five-foot drop-off, into some prickly bushes, and I lay there for six or eight hours. At first, I could see flashlights and police officers moving around. I was scared. Eventually, that went away, and I waited until it was light out before I dared to return to my apartment.

In the meantime, they searched my trunk and found the evidence that tied me to the electronics stealing at my own complex. I was caught.

Before I went to court, my parents and I discussed whether or not we should hire an attorney or get a court-appointed attorney. Looking back, I probably would not go with a court-appointed attorney again. You don't always get the best treatment in that situation. They just kind of want to get you through the whole process, and they might not always care for your best interest.

At the time we got arrested, my soccer coach called me and said I was off the team. I hadn't expected that to happen, but at that point, there were only a few games left. I wasn't going to classes, and I didn't have much to lose. I would have been kicked out of school anyway as soon as grades came out.

I pleaded guilty to burglary, was sentenced to thirty days of work release—which meant I stayed at the work release center—and three years' probation. On top of that, I had to pay about four thousand dollars in restitution for what I'd stolen. I'd gone to court free, and I left in handcuffs in front of my parents.

My college athletics career was over. I thought I didn't care and figured I'd have time to go back to athletics later, after my partying days were through. I had no idea of the remorse and regret that would haunt me.

Looking back

After my arrest, I could have decided to be a better person, but I chose to be a better liar instead. In each of our lives, we need an evaluation process. Obviously, I should have been thinking about the fact that my life was out of control. Instead, I was still angry about what had happened in high school. I still had a ton of options, but as most addicts do, I used my sports injuries as an excuse for my addictive behavior.

CHAPTER SEVEN
CANDY FLIPPING

If I were a soft drink, I'd be Jolt. I think Jolt best describes me because Jolt makes people wild, and I'm always wild. If I were a movie, I'd be Die Hard. It always keeps you on the edge of your seat.
—Mikael Luman, journal, September 9, 1988

I loved girls, and girls loved me. Lake Oswego Point opened the door to older women, who intrigued me if only because they were so different from the ones I'd known.

Diana and I were introduced at the club by another girl I knew. Diana was a nurse, older than I was, stacked and confident. Before that time, I'd only dated high school girls. Diana was a woman. Instead of an apartment, she had her own condo; she had the nice furniture, the nice wine and the nice crystal to serve it in. I felt weird but excited to be there with her. I thought she knew the truth about my real age. That was mistake number one.

"So how old are you?" she asked as we were lying together that night, after having sex.

"How old do you think I am?"

"Oh, about twenty-three or twenty-four?" she asked.

Stupidly, I told the truth. "I'm eighteen," I said with a big, proud, post-sex smile.

"What?"

Next thing I knew, I was standing in my boxers on the porch.

"You're telling me you didn't have fun?" I asked. "Does it matter if I'm eighteen, twenty-one or whatever? Can I at least get my clothes back, please?"

I really hadn't meant to deceive her. She'd wanted what we'd done as much as I had, and if I'd thought my age was going to be such a big issue, I would have told her upfront. But it was, and I hadn't, and that's how I happened to be standing in my shorts outside when I should have been back in bed with her. She took it personally, too, as I would find out later—she called the bar and told them my age.

XTC

Fortunately, Lake Oswego Point was becoming less and less important to me. When it closed up around two a.m., we didn't. I met a group of guys there who told us about Embers, an after-hours bar they went to that was open until four. They invited me to come along to do ecstasy with them.

My new friends said ecstasy was the only way to go—that I wouldn't have to drink as much and that it would intensify whatever I was feeling. That's all I needed to hear. This was on a Friday, so the plan was for me to do ecstasy with them the next night.

I was seeing Trisha, a girl who lived in my apartment complex. It was nice to have someone to go back to in case I didn't score that night—nice to have a booty call. I, of course, preferred to be alone with my friends, but that night, she was with me. The first half hour to forty-five minutes of the effects was pretty intense. I just sat there on the chair, my face dripping with sweat, my hair plastered down. The feeling was overwhelming, and it came on quickly. Trisha, who'd done it with me, was feeling the same thing. She sat on my lap, moving all over me, rubbing the sweat off my forehead.

I couldn't believe the feeling. It was the best I'd ever felt on any substance, and way more intense than being drunk. Besides, when I'd get drunk, I would do stupid stuff. I didn't feel the energy of the music or the atmosphere. Alcohol dulled everything, but taking ecstasy intensified everything outside and within me.

The first couple of times we went to Embers, I wasn't sure how I felt about it. A gay bar, it was full of street people and drag queens. On one of our early visits, Alex got into it with two gay guys, and we were immediately kicked out. Soon, though, we became more comfortable there—which, as I was soon to find out, was going to be a good thing.

Alex and I liked to dress up nice, so we would wear , black pants, expensive shoes and either a white or colored shirt with a patterned vest over the top. That's how we got the nickname "the Vesta Boys."

Ecstasy tasted terrible, but because I wanted to get higher quicker, I'd stick it under my tongue and let it dissolve. After a while, you get a sore under your tongue if you continue to do it, but I didn't care. I wanted to get as high as possible. It was the beginning of an attitude that developed as I became more addicted to drugs. It wasn't exactly suicidal. It was more a feeling of *If I'm going to die, oh well. Might as well die high and having fun.*

Although my experiences at Lake Oswego Point were intense to say the least, they lasted only about six months. Two factors contributed to that: ecstasy and my unfortunate one-night stand with the nurse.

I'd had surgery on my knee again. I went to the club with my friends, and we got there early, before seven p.m. The manager came over to me and asked to see my ID. That seemed weird, since I was a regular by then. I gave him the ID, and he said, "I'm going to have to ask you to leave."

"Why?" I asked.

"Because I don't believe that you're who you say you are."

He gave me the ID back, and I went back to the apartment to drink. My friends called me around two a.m. to come pick them up. I had to drive all the way back down to Lake Oswego Point, which took about thirty minutes. As I was leaving the club, I noticed a police car behind me. He pulled me over, and I got out of the truck. He asked why I was driving, since I had a knee brace on.

"Well, my friends were drinking," I said, "and they needed me to come pick them up." I wanted to make it sound like I was doing him a favor.

At that time, the manager from the club drove up. My guess is that he'd seen me pick up my friends and called the cops so that they'd pull me over and find out who I really was. I'd already given the police officer my real name, and the manager came over and said something to him. At that time, my license had been suspended for not paying tickets. As a result, I got a ticket for driving without a license and was charged with misrepresentation of age. With the help of a court-appointed attorney, I fought the charge in court. The judge dropped the case because I was in the club before eight o'clock, when minors were supposed to leave. Off the hook once more.

A couple of months later, when we were down at Embers, Nurse Diana's friend came up to me. She said that I'd gotten Diana pregnant, that she'd had an abortion and moved to Washington. She also said that Diana was the one who told the club manager about my age. She was one angry lady.

The after-hours group

By then, I didn't care about Lake Oswego Point. I'd met a new group of friends at Embers. I'd been doing ecstasy a little more than a month, and my new group of people—Bobby J., Doug-E, Eddie B. and Scooter—had been involved in the rave scene for about a year, and they were a lot more experienced.

Doug was the ringleader and the one who had the drugs. He'd invite us over to his house an hour earlier to drink carrot juice so the ecstasy would hit us harder. In the world of drugs, he was the motivator. He could make a good time a great time, and could get me into that groove I loved.

We'd go down to Embers, and afterward, party until four a.m. After the party, fifteen or twenty people would always go to after-hours with them at a house at Meikle and Burnside, where Kevin and Patrick—part of the new group—lived. At their day jobs, Kevin and Patrick sold furniture. We'd get mattresses out of the garage, bring them in the house, put them in front of the windows and crank the music. It was like a ritual, like being in our own little world. We'd party through dawn until seven or eight in the morning. Then we'd go home, sleep for a few hours and be back doing it the next night.

Ecstasy wasn't the kind of drug I'd do during the day. So all week long, I'd be thinking, *Gosh, I can't wait until next weekend to do ecstasy again.* As I was soon to find out, with speed, there isn't any break. You don't think, *I can't wait to do speed again* because you're doing it all the time.

High times

With ecstasy, every week was better than the last one. We'd keep asking ourselves how it could just keep on getting better and better, but it did. After the first four or five times, I started doing acid with ecstasy. It was called "candy flipping," and it was even better. The ecstasy made me kind of immobile, where I'd just want to sit there and touch and rub on people—which is more toward the heroin effect. Downers didn't appeal to me; I didn't do drugs to get down. I wanted to be up, running and jolting around. Drinking had partially done that for me, but once I started doing ecstasy, drinking didn't even make sense.

My usage increased by the day. I went from using one hit of ecstasy to using one and a half, to using two, to using acid. Inevitably, around that time, I also began to deal ecstasy. I didn't think of it like that, though—more like hooking people up. I always had drugs on me. If someone would want to buy half a hit, I tried to be Mr. Nice Guy, so I'd take the other half.

Trisha worked early in the morning on Sundays, so she'd always leave me at the bar around two o'clock. That gave me from two to four to do whatever. During the first couple of weeks, I went to after-hours with Kevin and Patrick. As was the case most of the time when we got to after-hours, we were already high. One particular night, I was watching a girl named Anna. She reminded me of the strippers at the club in Vancouver—more like a woman than the high school girls I was used to. She was thirty years old, probably five foot ten, tan, with dark hair and fake boobs. Knowing that she had my attention, she began dancing in front on me.

I continued to eye her from the couch, and she said, "Little boy, you couldn't handle me."

"There's nothing you can do to me that I can't handle," I said.

So, just like that, she jumped on top of me, bit down hard onto my neck, ripped both of my shirts open and proceeded to scratch my chest from the top going down—fake nails digging into my skin as if it were clay. My buddies were freaking, and they finally managed to pull her off of me. I was just sitting there with two ripped shirts, blood dripping down my chest and a huge bite on my neck.

"You are right," I said. "I *can't* handle you."

After that, she was friendlier to me and in the nonsensical world of drugs, we just never mentioned the incident again. Alex ended up getting together with her a few weeks after my strange encounter, but she didn't go into attack mode with him. Apparently, what happened with me was a one-time thing. I had no doubts that she was freaky, but as we always used to say, "The freakier, the better."

That night, however, I just knew that she was too much of a freak. We left her far behind and the next morning, Alex and I went back to our apartment. As was Trisha's habit, she stopped at my apartment before she left for work in the morning. She'd already gotten there and of course, I hadn't arrived yet.

You've got to picture this: Alex and I were walking from the parking lot, and we were saying something like, "Last night was great, the best night ever." As I've already said, on ecstasy, every night is better than the last one. I didn't even realize that I had both shirts ripped, scratches down my chest and bite marks on my neck. We walked around the corner, and Trisha stood aghast at the top of my stairs, staring at me.

Confused, I took two or three steps up toward her, but she started charging like she was going to tackle me. I took a couple of steps back, and she ran down the stairs and took off.

"Hey, what's up with her?" I asked Alex.

He broke up laughing and said, "Look at you."

I looked down at myself. I could see why she might be a little bit upset. Still, I—who was never faithful to any girl—had been faithful that night. With women, I just couldn't win. I didn't know then that I'd never be able to have a good relationship with a woman until I ended my relationship with drugs. Back then, I didn't even know I had a problem.

Ménage à trois

Another night, when Trisha wasn't at Embers, I noticed two girls dancing together. I'd seen one of them around before and liked her looks.

"Hey, want to dance?" she asked.

"Sure," I said and motioned to my friend, Xavier.

Soon, he joined us, and I was having a good time with the girls. I never really thought of myself as a good dancer, but when I got into that candy-flipping groove, I didn't care. I could feel it.

Sometimes I'd get frisky on the dance floor, but the girl would usually stop me before anything happened. Not this night. Before I knew what I was doing, I realized that I had my hands down the pants of both girls.

My friends stood on the catwalk, cheering. I knew that I'd gone as far as I could in public.

"Want to come back to our place?" I asked.

The girls eyed each other and shook their heads. "No," one of them said. "We want you to come back to ours."

Now that was promising. "Xavier and me?"

More shaking of the heads. "No. Just you."

I was nineteen years old. Xavier was twenty-eight, good looking, a skillful dancer. But who was I to argue? I happily got in the car with them.

One was married, she said, and out with her friend for the night. So maybe they were just joking around, I thought. From the center console, I began fooling around and undressing them in the car.

"Come on," I said. "How much did my buddies pay you to do this?"

Nothing, they insisted. No one paid them a dime.

When we got to the single girl's apartment, they asked if I'd like something to drink. Usually, I'd turn down alcohol, but the whole situation was kind of tripping me out, so I asked for a beer. The single one handed it to me, and they started up the stairs. I pounded the beer and followed.

The married girl headed to the bathroom. The other one pulled me to the bedroom. *Okay*, I thought. *Nothing weird, after all*. The married one was just going to use the bathroom and go to bed, right? Wrong. She soon appeared at the door, extremely upset when she saw that we'd started without her.

After sex, we lay there together, my head spinning. The two girls were hugging each other, and I wanted to cuddle too. I knew, though, that I'd better get home before Trisha arrived at my apartment. So, still unable to believe what had just happened, I put on my clothes and walked downstairs.

I was in Tigard, twenty miles from my apartment. My first lucky friend to get called to pick me up was Xavier. He was already upset because I went home with two girls without him, and he had no intention of rescuing me. Then I started walking, and called my sister. She wasn't there, but her roommate agreed to pick me up.

I was getting tired from all of the partying I'd done, so I sat down on sidewalk to wait. All of a sudden, I saw headlights shining in my face. I got into the car exhausted but proud of my accomplishment. After that, I gave my friends a hard time. I might be the youngest in the crowd, but I was the first to go home with two girls.

Jerry Springer, where are you?

Needless to say, none of these activities exactly strengthened my ties to Trisha. The relationship started to feel like too much baggage, and the advantage of booty call didn't outweigh the fact that Trisha could knock on my door anytime she wanted to. I wanted to be able to pick up on the other chicks. I wanted to party. I wanted to be available and, with so much sex all over the place, I didn't want a girlfriend in my apartment complex checking up on me every day. There were times she'd stop by when I had girls over, and I'd have to pretend no one was home. The girls knew, but when Trisha would call later and ask, "Where were you?" I'd say that I was sleeping or gone or out with my friends.

The week following my episode with the girls, we were down at Embers, and I knew that I really needed to get rid of her. But as with all of my relationships, I didn't want the confrontation with Trisha, and I didn't want to hurt her.

My older sister wanted some ecstasy, and she asked me to get it for her. I told her, "I'll give you ecstasy, all right, and I'll give you enough for you and for Trisha. In return, though, you've got to keep her away from me, okay?"

After two or three hours, I was still partying and realized that I hadn't seen them at all. Good riddance. At least my sister had done as I'd asked.

Embers had a catwalk up above the dance floor. I often watched a beautiful, aloof, dark-haired chick named Karen dancing up there with her roommate. Tonight, it wasn't that chick on the catwalk. It was my sister—and no, it couldn't be. But it was: my sister and Trisha doing some kind of weird dance. The next thing I realized, my sister and Trisha were up there making out. I'm not talking about "kind of" making out. They were all over each other.

Although it was a weird feeling to watch my sister with my girlfriend, it solved my Trisha problem. The story got even weirder, though. My sister and Trisha actually ended up moving in together. For about nine months, they were a couple. I couldn't believe it. But, yes, I was happy to get rid of Trisha, if only to my own sister. It was a Jerry Springer moment. I lost my girlfriend to my sister, and I was happy she'd taken her away.

The purple door

When the crowd from Lake Oswego Point started going down to Embers, the place went from a gay bar to a mixed bar. There were two different sections: the drag queens on one side and us on the other. We tolerated them, and they tolerated us. Often, we crossed sides as friends, sharing the same space, united by the common bond of drugs.

Candy flipping became my new favorite thing, containing all of the elements of a perfect high for me. One night, someone said there was a party at a club with a purple door. That's all we knew, but fueled by ecstasy and acid, we took to the streets anyway, yelling, "Where's the purple door? Where's the purple door?"

Doug, whom we called Doug-E, acted as if he knew where it was. I didn't know if he did, but I marched down the street as if I did. Sixteen, seventeen, eighteen, nineteen blocks later, we found the club, and there was the purple door.

The experience of entering that place was ten times weirder than the first time we'd gone to Embers. We'd gone from the cheerleader bar of Lake Oswego Point to the gay bar/rave scene of Embers, and now here we were with these people in their dark clothes, with huge holes in their ears. While it was provocative to watch two girls making out on the catwalk at Embers, there was nothing sexy about the sex behind the purple door.

Each addiction had taken me to a new environment, each one a little stranger than the one before. Although I didn't know it, the purple door was a symbol of the kind of people with whom I'd soon be partying.

Looking back

When your life is as out of control as mine was then, there's nothing that parents, teachers or friends can say to convince you to change. The consequences of this destructive behavior need to be taught at a younger age, before one is caught up, as I was, in the whirlwind of addiction.

CHAPTER EIGHT
GOOD TIMES FOR SALE

This stuff is so good, it should be illegal.
—Mikael Luman, 1993, on ecstasy

I'd always been afraid to dance, but when I was on ecstasy, the fear melted away. Sweat dripped off my face, and I hit the floor, dancing for hours on end. With candy flipping, I could feel the music, feel the beat. It was as if I had dancing shoes on. I was no longer interested in alcohol. With ecstasy, I'd start dancing at eleven o'clock at night. The next thing I knew, it would be six in the morning and my friends would be saying, "Mikael, we've got to go."

When we couldn't get ecstasy through one connection, I would start calling around to see where I could get it and before long, I had a couple of connections. Then, those connections started sending me down to Embers with drugs to sell. In my eyes, it wasn't dealing; I was just helping people have a good time.

One of my school friends said that one word that described me was "fearless." "Foolish" is more like it. There I was in the middle of the club, with a pocket full of drugs and a wad of bills, and I wasn't even worried about getting in trouble. It never occurred to me to be discreet about my conduct, because drug use was all over the place.

Your friendly neighborhood pusher

In the beginning, the motive was not profit but popularity and direct access to drugs. In fact, when I first started selling, it was probably costing me a couple hundred dollars of my own money. I was painting houses for my dad just to pay for selling drugs. I wanted people to like me, and dealing was my new sport.

I started buying ecstasy from Doug for my own use. He was one of those rare breeds who in spite of the ecstasy and the speed, went to school and worked full time. When he started supplying me with ecstasy to sell, I was buying it for twenty-three dollars a hit and selling it for twenty-five. As you may have noticed, that was a whopping two-dollar-per-hit profit. Doug told me he couldn't get it for much less and make a profit himself, and remember that I wasn't doing it for the money at that point.

I did enjoy the appeal of having the money in my pocket, whether it was mine or not. Until I gave it to Doug, I considered it my money, and I liked the way that felt. I was leaving a club one night, counting my money as I walked to my car in a parking garage. A guy and a girl pulled up next to me. The girl said something, and I leaned into the car. The guy reached across and grabbed the bills out of my hands, and then drove off. After that, I was more careful about where I counted my cash.

At that time, there were two different sources: Carter and Doug. The Lake Oswego Point group got hooked up through Carter. The Embers/rave group dealt with Doug. Carter was more out in the open about it and although Doug was quieter, he always had a stash. Later, I found out that Doug wasn't paying more than eight dollars a hit but at the time, I believed him when he said he couldn't sell it to me for less than twenty-three. That's what happens when you're raised by honest people. At that time, if you told me you were from Mars, I would have believed you.

My own consumption increased rapidly. I always wanted to get higher and higher and higher and do more and more and more. My needs escalated as the evening went on, and I always wondered if I could get just a little bit higher. Restraint was not a word in my vocabulary.

One night, I'd had about five hits of acid and five of ecstasy, and had gone with a girl who wanted to pick up some marijuana. The guy she bought it from had a big bag of mushrooms—which we called "shrooms"—and he asked me if I'd like some. He said it was kind of like acid but more earthy, and I was all for it. He tossed me the bag, and I was already so high that I just sat there eating the shrooms. The girl told me it was time to go, and the guy looked down at the bag and started laughing.

"Do you know how many shrooms you just ate?" he asked.

I felt bad and said, "Hey, would you like me to give you some money?"

"No," he said. "I just want to know what the experience is like."

By then, it was getting close to five a.m. We went to Kevin and Patrick's, and there were some people smoking marijuana. Although I didn't really like marijuana by itself, I sometimes smoked it after acid or ecstasy. When I was coming down, it kind of put me into another realm that I liked.

When they offered me some that night, I said, "Sure, I'll take a toke."

I took the hit, and it just put me in a different universe. All of a sudden, I was performing. It was the beginning of what would later be my stand-up routine. I didn't say anything at first. It started out with mime-type dancing. Then I kind of shifted into another gear and started doing a dance routine, and then people started just sitting down watching. Then, before I knew it, everybody—maybe thirty people—were watching. I was dripping with sweat and going a hundred miles an hour.

At one point, a girl asked Doug, "Should we take him to the hospital? Will he be all right?"

"He's perfect," Doug said.

I thought so too, but in reality, I was far gone. My act went on until ten or eleven the next morning. This was when I began to lose some of my insecurities about dancing.

Bobby J.

The first time I did an all-night, all-day party on ecstasy and acid was also the first time I met Bobby J. He was a surfer type with blonde hair, khaki pants and a cocky, been-there, done-that attitude. A good dancer, he never had to chase women the way the rest of us did; they always chased him.

Although we later became good friends, Bobby J. and I didn't hit it off at first. He was from the rave group, and I was from the Lake Oswego group. We went from Embers to after-hours at a girl's house. Everyone was doing a type of acid called Snowman. It was on little perforated pieces of paper with a snow-man printed on it. I did a hit of acid, then I walked with Patrick downtown—it seemed to take forever. We used to call it "hiking boots," because when you're on acid, you feel as if you can just go forever in those imaginary winged boots.

We went back, got more drugs, then returned to the after-hours house. It was morning by then, and we took some more acid. Then, we went out to Haag Lake, which was about a forty-five-minute drive.

I was driving with Patrick and Doug. On the trip out there, we did another hit of acid. It was about noon, and we'd been partying all night. There must have been a rally that day because for miles and miles, there were people on the sidewalk, holding up signs that said, "Stop abortion." We'd pass one group of them, and I'd think, *Good, we're past the "stop abortion" signs*. And then, here would come another group of them. They were everywhere.

We got to the lake, and Bobby J., Scooter and a couple of other people arrived in a different group of cars. That's when Bobby J. and I started to talk for the first time. I liked him and wondered how he'd gotten caught up in the drug scene. But then, who was I to judge?

Life on speed

The first time that I did speed, we partied on Thursday night and went back to Kevin and Patrick's. We did the same thing on Friday night. I was pretty worn out on that Saturday. My roommate, Alex, had gotten a girlfriend, and he was moving in with her. I was doing some painting work for my dad to make money. We were supposed to be out of our apartment on that Saturday. I didn't really know what I was going to do.

I slept in on that Saturday. I had just started a new job at the Olive Garden, waiting tables, and I was supposed to work on Sunday. I was going to take all of my bags to my parents' house. My dad had gotten tired of the tickets and my driving without a license and had taken back the truck.

I was singing the Eddie B. Blues that night. Eddie B. was always talking about how he wanted a different life, how he could be clean and sober. Whenever anyone in the group fell into a similar funk, we'd call it the Eddie B. Blues. Without a place to go, I put my work clothes in my backpack and went to the club. Daylight Savings Time gave us an extra hour. I'd already said, "I'm done using," but a guy I knew offered me some speed. He said it would give me energy, and I sure needed that. We went outside in his car and snorted it. I wanted to go right back in, but he said no, that it would drain, and we didn't want to walk around sniffing so that people knew what we were doing.

One moment, I was still exhausted. In the next moment, the feeling hit me in a burst. That invincible, on-top-of-the-world feeling I had briefly experienced with cocaine was back in full force and stronger than ever. Still high on speed, I went to where a new club, the Panorama, was opening up. Once inside, Karen, an attractive brunette my friends and I were all hot for, came up to me.

"Do you have anything for me?" she asked.

"What do you mean?" I said, "Ecstasy?"

She nodded. Of course, that would have to be the one night I didn't have any on me, but I didn't let that stop me. I got a couple of hits of ecstasy from someone else and gave one to her. We continued to party and went to after-hours together. Then we went to her house and talked nonstop for three hours. Not much of an open person, I was able to communicate with her that night the way I'd never been able to talk to a woman before.

The next morning, I showered and went to my new job at the Olive Garden. Tracy, a friend of mine who worked there, always liked to hear the tales of my wild life.

When I saw her that day, she took one look at me and said, "What have you been up to now?"

I couldn't control myself and said, "A gentleman never talks…so let me tell you all about it."

Looking back

When I substituted the clubs for sports, I told myself that I would get back to athletics sooner or later. In the meantime, I wanted to be the best partier, the best dancer, the best drug user, the best dealer. We always think that we're going to have time to do the things we really want to do, but we don't want to sacrifice the things that are fun to do. By the time it's no longer fun, it's too late to change.

CHAPTER NINE
SPEEDING UP

Everybody thinks I'm high, but I am.
—Mikael Luman on speed

After the first time I did speed, it was not like, *Okay, I do speed every weekend.* Ecstasy was still my preferred drug, and obviously, the combination of acid and ecstasy was what I really liked. When I met Karen, and even when we moved in together, I was still in the party mode, and it's not as if we met at a coffee shop.

Most of the girls I met, I slept with the first night. Karen and I did not have sex for three or four days, which was a first for me. That alone put me three or four days into the commitment. If I'd had sex with her that first night, and if I hadn't been staying at her house, we might not have ever gone out. But I was committed to finding a place to stay. And I was committed to at least have sex. For the first month or so, it was still fun because Karen would go out and party as hard as we would.

Just as Embers had replaced Lake Oswego Point, Panorama began to replace Embers. As far as my dancing went, I felt more confident in smaller groups, which was why I was able to let loose and get my groove at after-hours, where there were no more than twenty people. At clubs, I was more worried about getting attention and what people were thinking. Besides, I was selling ecstasy, so I was always doing something.

When we would go to raves, which weren't an every-weekend thing, there was more of an opportunity to dance. A rave doesn't get going until after midnight, when all of the drugs have already been sold and taken, so it wasn't like the selling of the drugs took away from partying. After I got together with Karen, the dancing and the partying got less and less, and the relationship overshadowed my own needs. All I wanted to do was dance all night, but all I ended up doing was sitting in the car with Karen.

One night, I insisted that we go inside, where the party was. Another girl, who was friends with both of us, was there that night, so that made it easier. We went to Doug's ahead of time and pre-partied. By the time we showed up close to midnight, I had a pretty good buzz going, and I took a couple more hits of ecstasy. I felt the music and was really in the groove. With drugs, a lot is timing. If the drugs hit at home, you've got to rebuild once you get to the club. But if they hit right as you enter the club, hear the music and start dancing, you get more caught into the progression. Before you know it, you're standing in front of the speaker and jolting. Pretty soon, all you can do is jolt.

Jolting, by the way, is hitting the beats. It's not as fluid as dancing, and I considered myself more of a jolter because I was wrapped up in the music and the moment and the drugs. It was always easier to get into that groove if I had someone with me. Doug was like that. He'd grab my hand, move everybody away from the speaker, and the next thing I knew he was jolting. When I partied with Doug, I had to have a focus, and I had to forget about the social aspect. He wasn't as gregarious as I was, but he was almost like a coach who was able to coax the last little bit of effort out of me. He was like the experienced veteran grabbing the rookie and saying, "Hey, you want to party? This is what it's really all about."

He was even more extreme than Bobby J. about the music. Tapes lined his wall at home, and he could tell you the location of where each rave was recorded. Doug-E was all about the music, and when I was with him, he wanted it to be all about the music for me, too. He literally dragged me in there, dragged me up to the front of the place and just started going at it. Once I started dancing, it was the same time the ecstasy started building. I'd just catch flashes, and next thing I knew it was two o'clock. Or I'd flash and someone would try to talk to me, but they couldn't break my bubble. The longer I was in that zone, the easier it was to dance. The first part was always the hardest. That night I felt one with the music. By four o'clock, I looked down and saw a cigarette butt in my curled fingers. I couldn't even remember smoking the thing. I kept on dancing.

Karen came up to me, trying to get me to leave. I wasn't leaving, though. She finally gave up and took off with her friend. She could have told me anything, and it wouldn't have mattered. I kept on dancing. The next thing I knew, it was morning. Light came in from the door. The overhead lights were all on. Although the music was still going, they were shuffling people out and cleaning up. But Doug and I were still right there in the groove. My ears were ringing with a loud, deep rumble in my head. People were telling us we had to leave, but all of my senses weren't quite registering. I could still feel the music even though they'd turned it off. I'd sweated so much that my socks were soaked.

The minute I walked out the door into that outside world, my first question was, "Okay, where else can we go to party?"

Doug was the same way. It had been so good up to that point that I didn't want to stop, because I didn't know if I'd ever get back to that place again. Karen was long gone, so we had to find a ride. By then, it was almost easier to dance than to walk. I'd been dancing so long, my muscles weren't used to walking. We ended up getting on a bus and going to an after-hours at the other side of town. Then we went back to Doug's place until he had to go to work that afternoon. After he left, I called Karen, trying to figure out how to salvage the relationship.

The raves were on Saturday night, and we'd start partying on Thursday night. So by the time the rave rolled around, we were pretty spun out. Everything hit us harder. At that point, it was tough for me to do anything but dance. We'd party from about midnight until seven or eight in the morning, and sometimes after that we'd have an after-hours party that lasted into the evening.

The relationship with Karen kept me from doing as much as I wanted to. I'd heard about after-hours at a club run by a guy named Trey, and I really wanted to go. Karen said that she did too, but we never ended up there.

When I first started doing crystal meth, between Daylight Savings Time and Christmas, I started having issues with my stomach. The doctor said it was irritable bowel syndrome, but for two or three weeks, my stomach was so sore that I couldn't party. I can remember going to Kevin and Patrick's house and everyone wanted to know what was wrong with me. I couldn't figure it out. My body was rebelling against the drugs, but my mind wouldn't listen.

High friends in low places
Bobby J. would often indulge in the Eddie B. Blues. A few years older than I, Bobby J. was kind of like I saw myself—a better person than he showed, always doing right to people who weren't necessarily doing right to him. I wanted to be like him.

At some time after we began taking speed, Bobby J. decided that enough was enough for him. So he checked himself into a detox center. Bobby J. had always said that he wanted to change, and that he couldn't continue living the way we were. I didn't get that way until much, much later in my addiction. He'd already gone to detox a few times, thinking that if he went for seven days, he could kick it. But he always ended up coming back and doing it again.

He called me from the detox place that night and said he really wanted some ice cream. They weren't supposed to get anything from the outside, but he told me where to go, and told me how to find the window to his room. I went and bought some ice cream and sneaked up to the detox center, making sure that no one saw me. The window was open a little, and I put the ice cream on the ledge. What I didn't know at that time was that down the road, I'd end up in the same place five years later.

Looking back

Even though I was visiting Bobby J. in a detox center, and even though I was addicted to speed, I really didn't know what addiction was. If you'd asked me, I would have told you that I was just having fun. It was fun at that point. It was a lot of fun. It kept me from thinking about the losses in my life, and it kept me from healing.

CHAPTER TEN
SMOKE 'TIL YOU'RE BROKE

You always jumped first, from the highest point and without hesitation. You made us wish there were more seatbelts in whatever you drove, and you certainly never failed to gain the affection of the ladies.
—J.D., a longtime friend

Cocaine was never my thing, but it was the drug that I could make money on. Since I didn't do coke, when I found out that my brother and his friends wanted it, I found a connection and sold it to them. When you have a supply, there are always potential buyers, and that's what happened with the coke. I was partying with Max, Trisha and Eddie B., and Max wanted some cocaine. I said, "I have some."

Before Bobby J.'s speed addiction, he had a bad coke habit. He and Max were there, and he wanted to sample it. It was my first experience smoking it. When I blew out the smoke, my knees were buckling, and there was a high-pitched ringing in my ears. It's called "chasing the dragon" because that's what you're doing. Once you blow it out and that feeling goes away, you want another hit.

After I took a few hits, it was like all of a sudden the coke had disappeared; we'd smoked a whole eightball. Once it was gone, we were looking for more—on the floor, in the cracks in the table. It's called "jonesing," and we were literally jonesing for more. I jonesed so hard that I broke the coffee table. All of the others there had already experienced this, so they were sitting there somewhat calm, while I was crawling around, searching the floor.

When we finally realized that there wasn't any more, I was so shocked and so stunned that we'd gone through my profits. I sent Max off with another eightball. Not long after, he came back wanting another. A few hours later, he returned again. After that I knew that if someone smoked coke, I'd make a pretty good profit. By the third or fourth time, I could sell a two-hundred-dollar eightball for four hundred dollars.

We always said, "Smoke 'til you're broke," and that was pretty much my attitude toward cocaine. Everybody thinks their addiction is better than the other one, and I thought speed beat coke. I could do a quarter gram of speed and be happy all night long. Coke's twice as expensive as speed, and the effects don't last nearly as long. At least with speed, you're able to pass the pipe to the next person. With cocaine, you don't want to, especially if there's a group of people.

Rollerblading

One night, we were downtown at a birthday party with a friend of Bobby J.'s. We were at his house, and Karen kept paging me. I finally called her back to see what was going on, and she said, "I want you to bring my car back."

"I'll bring it back to you in the morning," I said. "We're partying."

We argued about it, and finally she said, "You bring the car back tonight or there will be consequences."

I asked my friends who was going to follow me out to Beaverton, but no one wanted to.

"Fine," I said. "I'll just Rollerblade back here."

I dropped off the car, kissed Karen goodnight and said, "I'll see you tomorrow."

I'd started selling cocaine as well as speed and ecstasy at that time, and I remembered that my little brother and his friends liked coke. So I called him and asked him for a ride downtown. His excuse was that the transmission in the car was out and he couldn't drive it back up the hill.

I said that was fine, that he could just give me a ride to the top of Barnes Road. While I was waiting for him, I snorted crystal and got my Rollerblades ready. My brother picked me up. By then, I was pretty excited to do it. I'd told my friends I was going to, and it was almost a dare, in my mind at least.

At the top of Barnes Road, we were looking down. It was extremely steep, dark and narrow. I snapped on my Rollerblades and got out, and the kids were pretty worried. I put on my headphones, turned up the music and tried to figure out the best way to do it. So I started going down the hill. When you're wearing Rollerblades that don't have brakes on the back, the way that you stop is to cut back and forth. The road wasn't in very good shape, and its surface was pretty oily.

I was kind of cutting back and forth, but it got to a point where it was dangerous for me to do that. On most roads there would have been a side road coming into it, where I could shoot into and slow down. But not on Barnes Road. I got going so fast that there was a point where I just went into a tuck. It was about two in the morning, and I was flying. As I got closer to Portland, there were traffic lights, but I was going way too fast to stop at them. I went over the freeway and into the downtown area. At that point, I was kind of in my zone, focused on getting to where my friends were. I heard a car honk a few times, and although I didn't realize it at first, it was my friends. There were four of them in a VW Bug.

"Get in," they yelled.

"Where are you going?" I asked.

"To Kevin and Patrick's for after-hours," one of them said.

"No," I told them. "I'm going all the way."

My friends had to drop somebody off, and I continued to Rollerblade. I got in such a groove that I actually beat them to the house. It was the way I got when I was dancing. When I was in that kind of zone, I didn't realize that I was tired. Once I finally got to Kevin and Patrick's and knocked on the door, they asked how I'd gotten there.

"I Rollerbladed," I told them, feeling pretty smug. But after two or three minutes, it was pretty overwhelming, and I had to sit down. They were all freaking out that I was hurt or going to die or whatever, but I was just pretty exhausted. That's the kind of insane behavior that took over when I was on speed.

Speed and more speed

I worked at the Olive Garden from the time that I met Karen. Alex and another friend, Mack, also worked there. Usually we worked until about ten p.m. Then we were out of there in time to go party. Mack and I would always meet in the bathroom to do cocaine or crystal to get ready for the party.

There'd be times Mack would say, "Hey, watch my table." And he would actually go across the street to the Applebee's for happy hour. That's right. He had the nerve to actually head over there during his shift, have a drink, and then come back and continue to bus tables. Addicts are risk takers; we're already betting our lives. So what's a job?

By 1993, pagers were the new thing, and of course, I had one. My manager at the Olive Garden said, "Only drug dealers and businessmen have pagers. I don't like them at the restaurant."

"Aren't drug dealers businessmen?" I asked him.

With that attitude, it's no surprise, I guess, that my career at the Olive Garden was a short one—only about six or seven months. My dad had a lot of painting jobs lined up that spring, though, and the opportunity to paint houses was more appealing than working at a restaurant where I had to show up at a certain time. When I was working at the Olive Garden, I was still able to party and use speed on the weekends, and during the week, since my shifts were later, I was able to sleep until three or four in the afternoon. The painting jobs would start earlier, but I knew no one would complain if I slept in. I might not be on time for my painting jobs, but as I mentioned in an earlier chapter, I was meticulous, and my customers liked my work.

Looking back

Back then, I thought a dealer was someone who sold drugs to school kids or peddled them on the corner. What I was doing was just as bad, though. Coke was a nonstop, can't-stop drug, and I was fueling the fire. What was happening to my friends should have shocked me. Instead, I was excited when someone came back three times in a night for more; it meant more money for me. I wasn't the same person I'd been five years or even two years before. I was a dealer.

CHAPTER ELEVEN
ALL THE SPEED, ALL THE TIME

We couldn't paint houses without being loaded.
We couldn't even get off the ground if we weren't high.
Everyone says you'll get more done on drugs, but you really
get less done because you're spinning your gears.
—Artie, a longtime friend

There was a point in there somewhere when I came up with the bright idea that I was tired from partying and needed to go to work. But I still had the speed I used to party on the weekend. And I had the speed I sold. Enter bright idea. I'd just do a little bit of speed. That was the point that it changed from just doing it on the weekends to party to doing it all of the time, to maintain.

The problem with speed is that once you're doing it, it's tough to be doing anything if you're not doing speed. When you stop using it, obviously there's going to be a comedown time where you've got to sleep it off. When I came down, I came down hard. I wasn't one of those people who could do it for two or three days, then be okay and go to work. I literally had to sleep for two or three days, and even after that, I had trouble just getting up.

Part of that was mental, too. I was down and feeling depressed, so it was tough to motivate myself to get moving. When I got up in the morning, I didn't feel like I got into my mental groove until late in the afternoon, so speed helped me get up and get going. Obviously, when you're doing speed during the day, sleeping at night becomes an issue. We used to have a saying: "Work more hours, so you make more money, so you can buy more speed, so you can work more hours." It's kind of a vicious cycle. The more you do, the more you need, and the more you need, the more you do.

James, my high school friend, came back to town for a visit, and he and Aaron stopped by. I couldn't believe how far apart we'd grown in the short time we'd been away from each other. I showed speed to them, maybe half-hoping they'd want to partake, and they just shook their heads.

"What are you doing, dude?" James asked. "What's this all about?"

At that point, to me it was no big deal, but they'd never been around it. They were put off by it.

Sketchin' out

Partying with Karen became less fun for me. In a relationship like ours, there were different rules. We were partying when we met, and our relationship revolved around that. She wasn't a bad person. She had a good job and was the first girl I'd included in family events. Still, it was tough to be in a relationship when I knew all of the girls, and I was friends with all the girls and, not to mention, selling ecstasy to all the girls. There was a jealousy factor between Karen and the other girls too. If we'd both been clean when we met, the outcome of our relationship might have been different, but when addiction is the matchmaker in a love affair, there's only one outcome.

Karen and I had been partying all weekend long, and it was a Saturday, and everybody was down in the basement partying. The records were spinning. I was upstairs, waiting for some people to show up. Being on speed is called "sketching." When I first started doing speed, everyone would say, "Oh, you're sketching, you're tripping," but I didn't ever realize what sketching was until I did it myself. I'd never done the peeking-out-the-windows thing. But I did look out the window because I was waiting for some people to show up. Once I started, that was all I could do, just keep looking out the window. Then, as I continued to look, I thought all of the cars had people in them, and I kept thinking all parked cars had two people. Why wouldn't they get out of the cars and come party? I wondered. That was my introduction to sketching out.

 Bobby J. used to say, "Try to keep it under ninety." He always wanted to keep his life under ninety, but I didn't. It got to the point that I was high so much and heard music so much, that I could be working on a Monday and still hear the music playing in my head.

Although my license had been suspended for a few unpaid tickets, it didn't stop me from driving. And of course, I was pulled over. One time I was with Karen, and another time I wasn't. Both times, there were drugs in the car.

When Karen and I were pulled over, I was certain we hadn't been speeding. The officer came up, and I asked, "What's wrong?"

"Your tags are expired," he said.

That didn't make sense either. "When did they expire?" I asked.

He gave me a date later than the present one. This was July, and he was telling me they expired in November. When I questioned him on it, he said, "I could have pulled you over because you have your license plate lights out."

I'd just replaced the light, and told him so. Then I got out of the car to show him.

"Oh, okay," the cop said. Then he got back in the car and drove off.

All he had to do was search the car, and I would have gone directly to jail. But maybe jail wouldn't have helped me then. I had many more lessons to learn.

Still shots

At some point, Karen and I were no longer able to go out and party together. We'd get down to the party, and I'd be all ready to go inside and dance all night. Just as I was ready to get out of the car, Karen would say, "We need to talk."

Anyone else would have said, "F—- you. Get out of the car," but I'd never been able to handle the down side of relationships because I didn't want to hurt anyone or deal with conflict. Besides, Karen was decent, and I cared about her. Thus, there were plenty of nights that we would sit in the car and talk all night long until six in the morning, when I'd finally be able to go inside and start partying.

"Hey, Mikael, good party," my friends would say. "Too bad you couldn't even get out of the car."

In spite of the problems, it was tough for me to leave Karen because I cared about her as a person. It was a codependent relationship, but it was my relationship, so I hung on as long as I could. There was a party at the beach that I wanted to attend. Karen didn't want to go, but I convinced her that I should. Doug-E, Bobby J. and Eddie B. had all come over to pick me up, and I was all dressed and ready to leave.

Even though Karen had said I could go, when my friends got to the door, she changed her mind and said she wanted me to stay home with her. Why would Karen always say I could go do something, and then at the last minute say I couldn't?

My friends were getting eager to leave, so I told them to go get in the car and give me two minutes.

Karen decided that she was going to stand in front of the door so that I couldn't leave, but that wasn't about to stop me from partying. I jumped over the couch, opened up the back door, went out on the patio and jumped over it. We were on the second floor, and it was wet outside. I caught my foot and kind of landed on my side in the wet, muddy grass. After scrambling to my feet, I started running out toward the parking lot to catch my buddies. No sign of them, so I ran across the parking lot, up and down a hill through some trees.

Still no sign of them, and it was less than two minutes from the time they left. It was no fun having to go back to the apartment. The front door was locked, of course, and I had to knock on it and make my apologies. Karen wasn't happy that I'd been willing to jump the balcony to get out for the night. I went inside, changed clothes and showered. Then I finally talked her into letting me go and paid my little brother's friend to drive me.

There was another incident when Karen accused me of kissing a girl at the club. I think this was the changing point with us. It was one of those times when I was out of touch with reality, when I'd done way too many drugs, and there was a portion after about eleven o'clock that I forgot. The next thing I knew, it was morning, and we were at after-hours at Kevin and Patrick's. When I was that gone, people always tried to fill in the blanks, and my mind was no longer a camcorder with a constant picture. All I could drum up were still shots. Karen explained the incident where she saw me kissing the girl, and I had a still image of it because of what she explained—but not necessarily an image of it ever happening. I truly believed that she invented it, either because of her own impairment or maybe just as a reason to argue. Either way, I think that maybe in her head that might have been the changing point as well. Living together wasn't fun anymore, not for either of us.

Looking back

Justification is a major part of addiction. I justified dealing drugs at the club by telling myself that I was just hooking people up. I justified my addiction to ecstasy by saying that I did it only on the weekends. I even justified selling my brother drugs because he was already using them and would have gotten them anyway. I justified my everyday speed use because I thought that I needed it to function. The bottom line is that there is no justification for that kind of behavior, and until you recognize it as a thinking error, you are going to continue to use it in all aspects of your life.

CHAPTER TWELVE
NONSTOP PARTY

It's really difficult to be in a relationship and loving someone
when they pick another person over you. But it's worse when
what they pick over you is a thing, a drug.
—Karen, a former girlfriend

Bobby J., Doug and I decided to see how long we could party without mundane stuff like sleep. I'd gotten the green light from Karen, so from Thursday through Sunday, we partied. That Sunday, Bobby J., Eddie B. and I walked to the grocery store. Most of the time I thought I looked pretty presentable, but if the way Eddie B. looked when he took off his sunglasses was any indication of my state, I didn't want to know about it.

"Put your glasses back on and clean your eyes," I told him, and hoped I didn't look a fraction that bad.

Karen was at Doug's house when we got there. She took one look at me and said, "You're going home." I was almost to my Sunday night goal, and there was a rave that night I wanted to go to.

"One more night," I said.

"No way. You are in no condition to party tonight."

After thirty minutes or so, I agreed to go back to the apartment with her. *If I can't party, at least I'll have sex*, I decided. We pulled over at the cemetery, got naked and had sex. Then we went home and continued. I slept until about eight p.m. but I was still pretty spun out. My friend Brody was supposed to pick me up, but he took one look at me and said, "No, you're going straight to bed."

Brody came from a family with money and was spoiled rotten growing up. He'd been in the military for a couple of years and thought he was a lot cooler than he was. We were friends for the most part, but the real reason we remained friends was because we were always competing with each other.

Renaissance man

Two of the most popular European DJs, Sasha and Digweed, were going to be in town. Everybody had their CDs, but we'd never seen Sasha and Digweed live. I planned for this party for weeks. My grandfather had a bomber convention in Savannah, Georgia, and I'd agreed to go with him on Monday morning. The party was on a Saturday night, and it was everything I'd expected. Randy, the financial backer of the rave, invited us to go to his house for after-hours. He was a jerk, but we kind of clicked because we were both smartasses.

He had a ten-foot bong. I was already messed up on acid and ecstasy. There weren't many people wanting to take on that bong. You'd have to sit on one side of the bed, and the bong would go across the bed on the floor. Someone had to light it. The objective was to get as much smoke in there as possible. I took one hit and coughed for about an hour and a half. Randy and I were the only ones who attempted it.

I was in another world, and it wasn't a perfect world. I was wandering around Randy's house unable to be still. Although I would experience it later, this was the first time I felt like there were two different languages being spoken in the same room. The only person I could talk to was Randy. Anything I said to anybody else sounded like gibberish. We hung out until ten that night. No one else in the house even knew what we were talking about, but Randy and I were in that same zone.

Karen dragged me out because she knew I had to get ready to go with my grandpa. I wasn't looking forward to a week with him at a bomber convention. He was in charge of a souvenir booth at the convention, and four came really early that next morning. Still I dragged myself to my grandparents' house and slept all the way to the convention.

After having dinner with my grandpa that night, I went to bed early but was still dragging. He was in the early stages of Alzheimer's, and he was really struggling with the paperwork and the money. I offered to take care of that so that he could spend his time with his bomber buddies. Every time I sold something, I put half in my pocket, so I ended up skimming about twenty-five hundred dollars off the top. This was the first time I stole from anyone I knew, but I justified it by thinking that I was stealing from my grandfather, not the bomber group. I felt I deserved it because I was doing all of the work.

I had a bad cigarette habit by this time and wanted to keep it from him. Every few hours I'd say I had to go to the bathroom, but I'd really have a cigarette. He might have had Alzheimer's, but he wasn't stupid. By the end of the week, he said, "Look, Mikael. You don't have to hide your smoking, although I don't think it's the smartest thing for you to be doing."

Throughout my relationship with Karen, Brody and I remained friends. When I first met him, he was growing marijuana in his closet and also selling pounds that he was getting elsewhere. It was called "dirt weed" because it wasn't very expensive or very pretty. He was living with a girl, and when they broke up, he brought about a dozen plants over to our house for three or four days until he found a house of his own, where he turned that dozen into a hundred. Someone turned him in, and the cops raided his house and confiscated all of his marijuana. He wasn't arrested; they just gave him a court date. Brody continued to deal as if nothing had happened.

About this time, there was a big ecstasy bust in Portland, the biggest in the history of Oregon, and about two thousand hits of ecstasy were confiscated. That's about fifty thousand dollars' worth of ecstasy. Carter, one of the two primary sources in Portland, was arrested. That left only Doug. It also left Carter's girlfriend, an exotic stripper named Dee.

Free man

I'm sure it will come as no surprise for you to learn that my relationship with Karen did not work out. When both members of a couple are addicted, it's tough for one of them to stay clean. If one of them is getting high, the other person is too.

I don't think I ever said, "Hey, I don't want to be with you anymore," point blank like that. But I was tired of staying in the car with her when everyone else was partying. So, when the lease ended and it came time for us to move out of the apartment, I gave her money, and she ended up renting a room in a house up the street from where we were. I was all for it because I felt that if I was separated from her physically, I was that much closer to being on my own.

Since I'd given Karen the money to move, I didn't have a lot left. But when my grandparents moved into a smaller house, my grandmother gave me a complete, ceramic Department 56 New England village that I'd used to set up for her over the holidays. I ended up selling it for about twelve hundred dollars—

about a tenth of its total value—and I used the money to party. I don't like admitting that now, but it's the way I thought. The need to party was stronger than what I knew was right.

After partying, I was down to my last couple hundred dollars and I needed money and drugs fast. Brody was dealing speed and I bought half of an eightball from him for about seventy-five dollars. I split it into seven quarters and charged twenty-five dollars apiece. I was able to double my money, after using one of the quarters myself to get high. That was pretty easy. Next, I bought a whole eightball and sold it. Then, I bought a couple of eightballs, and sold them. I was pretty aggressive about going out there and selling it, telling all of my friends, as if I'd just gotten a new job. This was the beginning of my heavy dealing.

Looking back
It's not that I didn't love Karen. I just loved partying more. Relationships aren't going to keep you clean. They're especially not going to keep you clean if both people are using. It doesn't matter how much somebody loves you. They can't do it for you; you have to do it for yourself. Years later, after we were both clean, Karen and I made our peace. She was the first woman I'd loved with whom I could envision a future, but our love was doomed by drugs from the night we met.

CHAPTER THIRTEEN
DEALING HEAVY

1. I believe that every person should be in shape.
2. I believe that every person should play a sport.
3. I'm a person who is always active.
4. I'm a person who likes spending money.
5. I'm a person who likes to earn money.
—Mikael Luman, journal, September 13, 1988

Karen's next stop after me was Randy, which surprised me because she always said that he was a jerk. I was pretty sure it was a get-even thing, but I was just happy to be free of the responsibility of living with a girl—even a girl I'd loved. After breaking up with her, I didn't have a place to stay and was going from house to house. For a couple of nights, I stayed with Ted and his wife, and that's where I ran into Craig, who'd just gotten out of jail.

Craig was a hustler, a good salesperson, a fancy dresser, but extremely gullible and bad things just seemed to happen to him. If you looked at him, you'd think he was gay, but I don't think he was. His favorite expression was, "You know what I mean?" which used to frustrate me because if I'd known what he meant, I wouldn't be asking him in the first place. He's the one we named the "C nose" because he always had drugs around the outside of his nose. That's just the kind of person he was. None of us wanted to have the "C nose."

Dealing drugs brought about lifestyle changes for me. Ecstasy was sold on the weekend. Speed was sold all of the time. When I first started, I was helping Brody. We had done some other dealing in the past, so this wasn't my first time working with him.

We never knew who gave the police the information that led to Carter's drug bust for ecstasy, but for years after that, everybody thought that it was Brody. Regardless of whether or not it was true, the end of the old connection provided a golden opportunity for him. Brody took full advantage of it and got a California connection for ecstasy. An ounce was selling for about three thousand dollars. Brody would fly to California, and I'd go around all night pre-selling hits so that I could wire him more money to purchase it when he got there—the more you can buy, the cheaper the price you get. At the same time that I was out rounding up money for ecstasy, I was selling crank.

Once the word got out about me, people started to approach me with their connections. So, I was working for Brody, selling crank, and I was also looking for sources for bigger volumes of crank.

Club Paradise

I met Dee at an after-hours party. I'd seen her at her boyfriend Carter's house way back when I was getting ecstasy through him. She was five foot four, half Puerto Rican, a hundred and five pounds with double-D fake breasts you could see from behind. Of the few times I saw her prior, when she wasn't on stage, she wore loose clothes and didn't flaunt her body. After I met Dee, she introduced me to her best friend, Trey.

Trey owned a strip bar, and he was the one who'd gotten Dee to start dancing, before the fake boobs and before I met either one of them. The bar had been a success, but when he sold it, opened another and got more into drugs, the second bar never reached the success of the first. He was about the same height as Dee and kind of looked like Mario in the Mario Brothers video game. He had long hair in the back, cut in a mullet, and he always carried a gun.

His dad, Pinkie, was an inch or two taller. At fifty-five, Pinkie looked like he was eighty, balding on the top, with shriveled skin, and a gray ponytail down his back. His uniform consisted of tattoos, leather chaps, dirty jeans, t-shirt, leather vest and of course, a bowie knife.

Trey's bar was made up of two different worlds. He had the upper-middle class party crowd that hung out there, and interspersed with them were Pinkie's biker friends. A bunch of us would be partying, then kind of do a double take as a random biker guy filtered through. The first time I wondered who let these guys in from the streets. Then I discovered that Pinkie was Trey's dad. I couldn't believe it. He'd been an addict since Vietnam and wasn't a bad guy once I got to know him.

One of Pinkie's biker friends was named Chris. He was shorter and stockier than Pinkie and about the same age. We called him Chris Cross because he was supposedly a hermaphrodite. Yet he had kids. We hired a girl to fool around with Chris to verify that there were both parts there. She confirmed the story, but it's too gross to repeat in detail.

One night, long after closing, I heard a noise outside the bar. When I went to investigate, I realized it was coming from a small four-by-four cabinet. I opened it, thinking an animal was inside. It was an animal, all right—one of Pinkie's friends who had fallen asleep there. I shook my head. There are just so many times, in that life I once lived, that I had to ask, "Why?" I asked it plenty of times back then. I never got an answer.

Even though Trey had drugs, he wasn't obvious about it. I had no idea that he had a supply. I was getting drugs from Brody, and I figured I could impress Trey by offering him some.

"Hey, Trey, I'm going to do a line," I said. "Can I use your office, and do you want one?"

He said sure, and we did.

After a few times, he figured out that he could trust me. He'd say, "Hey, Mikael, I've got a little bit of stuff. Would you like to try it?"

That was the next step. He didn't come out and say he was selling it. He'd put it out there, and I'd ask if he could get any more of it and how much it would cost if I wanted an eightball.

Brody, on the other hand, was getting only ounces at a time, and the quantity wasn't where I wanted it to be. I didn't want to be hooked up by Brody; I wanted to hook Brody up. When I started getting drugs from Trey, that's when business really picked up.

"I'll hook you up," Trey said, "but don't you ever tell Brody where this is coming from."

In spite of Brody's persistent questions, I never did.

In the meantime, Daniel, a guy I knew from Embers, and I got a place at The Meridian—a nice apartment complex up on a hill. One day, Craig came over, high as he could be, wearing his usual nostril halo of drugs. He owed me some money, and as usual, his solution to owing me money was to convince me to spend more. He said that he could get some great stuff. I asked if he was on the stuff right then. He said yes, and I said, "I want some out of that, because you're way out of control."

I gave him a thousand bucks over and above what he already owed, and he left. Four or five hours later, he came back just as wound up and excited as when he left. He flipped the dope down on the ground where I was sitting. I grabbed the bag, opened it up and couldn't believe what I saw.

"It's powdered sugar," I said.

"What?" He was clearly shocked.

"Who'd you meet up with?" I asked.

At this time, the group to stay away from was the biker group, and this reeked of their antics. I asked him if he sampled it, and I soon figured out that they'd done a switch on him. Craig's luck remained as constant as the ring around his nose.

Looking back

The people in my life then were completely different than the friends I'd had in high school, but I still considered them good people. I treated them as friends and didn't question that they would treat me the same way in return. I thought I was put in that group in order to help them. In reality, I couldn't even help myself.

CHAPTER FOURTEEN
BIG-TIME CONNECTIONS

You actively sought greater and more spectacular tests of your limits. It always seemed to me that you did so more out of curiosity than a desire to impress. But it did impress.
—J.D., a longtime friend

When Karen and I first broke up, I immediately began partying, of course. Then, my life became more about the dealing and the money. Although I continued to party, I wasn't living for that alone any longer. I'd run around and sell to a few new people, then hit the club at one or two a.m. and go to after-hours. The focus was on getting all the selling done before going to party.

My drug connections went from Brody to Trey, and then from Trey to Hank, who was hooked up with some Mexican guys who were dealing drugs out of Woodburn. Hank was about six feet tall, with blonde hair and a hard-edged, get-to-the-point attitude. More your typical hardcore drug pusher, he was ruthless—the kind of person you'd see selling drugs in a schoolyard.

When I first met him, I didn't know that he was the one supplying Trey. Instead of Trey meeting me, Hank would meet me, and they let me believe that Hank was getting the drugs from Trey. I didn't put two and two together until much later.

With the exception of about one month, I never saw Hank in a house. He was either staying at a hotel, driving around in his Expedition or staying at his girlfriend's. He was one of the toughest I'd met in the drug business thus far. One day he was cleaning out his gun, and it went off. All of us in the room started feeling ourselves to be sure we weren't hit. We were okay, but a chunk of Hank's finger was missing. The gunshot had taken off the flesh right down to the bone. We were all in shock, but he didn't freak out. Since he couldn't risk a trip to the hospital, he just dumped alcohol on the wound and left it open to heal. That's the kind of guy he was.

Trey and a couple of other guys were friends with Carter, Dee's boyfriend dealer who got busted for ecstasy. They put money together and sent it down to Carter's California connection. The California guy didn't pay them, so Trey and a few other guys went down there to find him and get their money. Trey told Hank that, in his absence, Hank could just continue hooking me up with the drugs I was getting. That's not what happened though.

Faking the funk

When I was in the relationship with Karen, there was time when enough speed was enough, and it was time to go to sleep. For her, that is. Not for me. She didn't want to admit to herself that I was taking drugs all day, and it was no fun for me when she was sleeping, and I was bouncing off the walls. At some point, a girlfriend wants to do the relationship/cuddle thing. It's no fun lying there, pretending to be asleep, eyes wide open, faking the funk, as Bobby J. and I later called it, because I didn't want Karen to know I'd done speed before I'd left work. Those were some long, long nights.

Then we broke up, and I didn't have anything holding me down but quantity. When I started the heavy dealing, I had no girlfriend, an endless supply and no restraints. I didn't like staying at other peoples' houses, but if I did drugs for five or seven days and didn't sleep and crashed on someone's couch, I didn't care. By the time I was awake and realized I was on their couch, I was already doing more drugs. There was a time I stayed up for twenty days, nonstop. If I sat down, my eyes would close, but five or ten minutes later, I'd be at it again.

Hank was so impressed with how much I was selling that he started giving me better deals than Trey was giving me. In the meantime, Trey didn't just demand money from the California connection; he was involved in kidnapping him. They'd waited in front of the guy's house for two days. When they saw him going in, they grabbed him and pulled him screaming into the car. A neighbor called the police and told them what had happened. We'd heard that Trey could serve ten years, and we didn't know if we'd ever see him again. However, he returned within weeks. My guess is that he told the police that the guy was a drug dealer. By the time he got back, I was dealing in quarter pounds with Hank, and Trey got cut out of the action.

Dee was looking around for a replacement for Carter, the guy who'd been busted for ecstasy. I found it kind of weird that she liked me. Yet one night, she told me that she had double-D boobs, and I said, "Show me." She did, and that was the start of one of the most destructive relationships of my life.

I used Dee at first as kind of a booty call. I was always out running around, selling drugs. Dee worked until two-thirty, and after that, she'd go over to her girlfriend Annie's and want me to meet her. I'd always tell her I'd be there at three p.m., but it always ended up being five or six o'clock by the time I got there. Once I finally got with her, we'd have sex, and I would pass out for a day. It was twenty-four to thirty-six hours before I was back up and moving around again. Not the beginning of a great love affair, and it only got worse.

Failed intervention

It was only a matter of time, I guess, before my parents would discover evidence confirming what they already suspected. I tried to be careful, and with logic that made sense to me at the time, I carried my drugs around in a purse. If I ever got pulled over, I'd just say it wasn't my purse; that was the rationale. When I'd begun the heavy dealing stage, I was in the relationship with Karen and used her car. When we broke up, I lost my transportation. That meant I needed to borrow cars from my friends, including a girl I knew. That's about the time I hatched the purse plan.

I was doing a painting job with my dad when my friend Craig wanted to use the car. I let him have it and took the purse and put it inside my dad's Land Cruiser. We were inside, and my dad told me he had to go home to get something. I didn't think about it until right after he was out the door, and then it hit me. He was going to wonder whose purse it was. Would he look in it? I was stressing the whole time he was gone.

When he came back, he said, "We need to talk."

And I said, "Sure, we do."

He wanted to dump the drugs down the toilet, but at that point, I couldn't let that happen—because I was an addict, yes, but also because I didn't want to lose the money. I came up with some excuse about getting beat up if I didn't deliver the drugs. He actually gave them back to me.

Not long after that, my parents called me over to their house. These two guys my parents knew from people in the church were there when I arrived. They guys explained that they'd been to prison for selling cocaine. I sat down, and they told me their whole story, about how sorry they felt and how they wished they'd never done it. I was still lost in the excitement of the heavy dealing, and their warning went in one ear and out the other.

The great motorcycle chase
One day Hank picked me up on his motorcycle, and we started heading to Beaverton, where I had another paint job. Hank had been on bikes since he was three or four years old, and he rode a motorcycle as if he were walking. I felt comfortable with him, and our trip was quick.

Then he made the mistake of cutting in front of a pickup, and it tried to sandwich us between it and another car. We were in the right lane at a red light. Hank and I had pulled the visors up on our helmets, and we were talking. There was a lane to our left, and there was also a right turn lane. The Nissan pickup we'd just cut off pulled into the turn lane next to us, and the driver spit in Hank's face. Not a good idea.

Now, Hank was a big-time drug dealer, so he always carried a gun and wasn't afraid to use it. The light turned green, and the pickup took off. We took off right behind it. The pickup slammed on its brakes, Hank did the same and we almost crashed into the back of the pickup. This happened a couple more times. Hank had gotten out his gun, but he was still trying to steer. I told him to give it to me so that I could shoot the guy, but Hank was adamant about doing it himself. The adrenaline had just taken over. I'd never even thought about shooting anyone, but at that moment, if the gun had been in my hands, I think I would have.

The pickup finally turned into the left turn lane and stopped at the light. Hank slowed down and bounced some bullets off the side of it. We kept going straight, not realizing that he had pulled back behind us. Either the guy was really stupid, or he had a bigger gun than we did. At the next intersection, I looked behind us and saw the pickup about ready to ram us. I hit Hank on the back, and shouted, "Go!" and we turned left toward the area where my apartment was.

A school bus was up ahead. We passed it on the right and the truck couldn't get by. Then we pulled into my complex and lost him. My apartment was up on the hill, so we could oversee the intersection. There were police cars but no signs of the pickup. Hank didn't really want to get back on the motorcycle, and I told him that maybe he should leave it with me.

Later on, Hank called me about midnight and asked if I could bring the bike out to the strip bar where Dee worked.

"Sure," I said.

"Have you ridden a motorcycle before?" he asked me.

"Oh, yeah," I said. "I ride them all the time." I'd only ridden once, and that was only up and down the street, so I had no experience with driving a motorcycle. Still, I wanted to ride this one.

Big talk, except that I couldn't even start the thing. So I had to call him back and ask him why it wasn't starting.

"You have the kickstand up, right?" he asked.

"Of course I have the kickstand up." Lie number two. I didn't know you had to have the kickstand up for the bike to start.

It was like learning to drive a car with a stick shift for the first time. I took the back way to the freeway and tried not to come to a complete stop so I wouldn't have to go through the gears all over again. Once on the freeway, I was going ninety to ninety-five miles an hour. I took a corner, starting off in the left-hand lane, edging toward the middle and then the far right side. I barely kept it from going off the road, but on the straightaway, I got it back up to speed going about one-twenty—thinking it was pretty cool.

I got to the strip club and parked the bike. As I was getting ready to walk inside, a woman pointed at me and yelled, "That's one of them. That's one of them right there." Turns out that about ten minutes before I got there, Hank and Santos decided they were going to teach some dude about respect. After he had mouthed off to them during a game of pool, they followed him into the bathroom. Once inside they brutally beat him with pool cues and then they took off on Santos' motorcycle.

"I don't even know what you're talking about," I said. "I just got here."

The bouncer at the strip bar made me stay until they could verify that I hadn't been involved in the restroom episode. After talking to Dee a little, I got yet another call from Hank. This time he wanted me to bring his bike down to the Copper Penny. Again, I couldn't start the bike. Sure I didn't have the kickstand up again, but more so because I was so shaken up, I wasn't even thinking about the stand. Finally, I managed to take the bike where he was.

After the experience of riding, despite the incident at the bar, I decided that I needed to get a motorcycle. If I was going to be out running around, selling drugs, I knew that a bike was the way to go. I was turning a half pound to a pound every three days, building up money.

Looking back

Until then, I'd only been hanging out with friends and partying at clubs. Now I was part of the drug-dealing scene, where anything went. Instead of freaking me out, it made my situation even that much more appealing. The rush of the lifestyle was just as addictive as the drugs.

CHAPTER FIFTEEN
IF YOU PLAY, YOU PAY

We both grew up in strong families and knew what we were doing was wrong. There were times when I was with Mikael that I was scared for my life.
—Artie, a longtime friend

When I got into heavy dealing with the crank, and I was probably selling quarter and half pounds, I got introduced by my contacts to the clients we called "the dykes"—an overweight couple I wish I'd never met. I had great gay clients, and at the clubs, I liked hanging out with the cute lesbians. The dykes were something else though. It was worse because they pretended to be my friends. Still, they sold quite a bit of drugs for me, and for a short while, it worked out well. One of the first times that I visited their home, I met Joseph, a gay guy. I liked him as I liked most people. I was talking to Joseph when I was over at the dykes' house, and he had mentioned something about having connections to get kilos of crank and cocaine down in California. I was still getting my crank from Hank and Santos in Woodburn but was always interested in new sources.

I figured if I could find a cheaper coke connection, I could make money off them instead of the other way around. I wanted to be the top person. I had overheard Hank and Santos talking about wanting to get kilos of cocaine. I asked them how much they were willing to pay. The most they said they could afford was twenty thousand a kilo.

I went to Joseph and asked him if he could get a kilo of cocaine and for how much. He said, "I don't know. Let me go check." Instead of getting back to me with a price, he said, "Okay. Kilo's en route. Be ready with the twenty-six thousand dollars."

I didn't know much about quality or quantity. Joseph justified the price by saying the quality was so pure you could cut it in half. But, I was taken aback because I'd never said I wanted it.

"We need to come up with the money or it's my hide," Joseph said. The only way to fix it was rounding up the twenty-six thousand for the coke. The dealers needed it by midnight, and it was already about four o'clock in the afternoon, so it was a bit of a stretch for me. Besides, I played on the city league softball team and had a game that night. I brought all of the drugs I had over to the dykes' house. I then called all of the people I knew, trying to get money for the coke. I was pretty confident that I could do it just as I had in the past, with Brody. My first thought was to call Hank and Santos. But they didn't want to pay the twenty-six thousand dollars. So they were out. That was fine. I wanted it for myself if it was that pure and I knew I could cut it in half and sell to Hank and Santos in the end anyway.

I left meth, marijuana and cocaine at the dykes' house. Then, I went to the softball game, and when I got back, we were being pressed for time. At about ten-thirty p.m., the dykes went from nice to pissed off. I hadn't even asked them to help, but when they heard about the purity of the product and the profitability, they thought the same thing I did. They got themselves involved. They took my drugs and my money and told me to get out of their house. What was I going to do? I went back to Hank and Santos because I didn't know what else to do. Once I explained what had happened to them, they wanted to know where the house was so that they could go get my stuff back.

I'd been on a motorcycle with Hank. I knew he wasn't joking. Santos wasn't joking either. I'd seen all of these guys outside our bar. I knew how fast they could draw their guns. No one ever shot, but it was pretty scary. That wasn't the solution I was after. I just ate the loss. I didn't want to see people get hurt.

I called the dykes over and over again. They clearly didn't want to talk to me. So I called Joseph.

"Don't do anything drastic," he said. "I'll work with it and try to get your money back. Just trust me."

If Joseph didn't have the money for the coke, then why didn't Joseph get in trouble? I don't know for sure if Joseph was ripping me off, the dykes were scamming me, or both of them together. I just know I was ripped off.

Before that, if I wanted to sell drugs to Joseph, I had to go through the dykes because the dykes and Joseph were friends. Then Joseph started calling me, and I started selling him crank. This went on for almost a month before he finally convinced me to send him down to California with some money. Obviously, I was a little cautious after what had happened with the dykes. I finally decided to trust him one last time.

Joseph was the kind of guy that in a normal life or even the one I was living, I should have for a friend. He'd graduated from Brigham Young and was a CPA, and I thought we had a connection because we were both raised Christian. He was also gay. Joseph asked me for cash because he was going down to California to make a buy. I gave him four thousand dollars—half of the amount he needed. He didn't come back when he was supposed to, and I figured he'd ripped me off, which had happened before. So I took the money I'd planned to give Joseph and bought a motorcycle. Made perfect sense at the time.

Seven days later, Joseph called me and said, "I'm right down the street. I've got the stuff. Do you have the money?"

I told him I didn't have the money because he'd promised to be back in three days, and he didn't have the greatest credibility. He was angry when he came to my house. I told him if he'd give me some time, I'd round up the money. Still, I'd already paid for half of the dope, and I wanted it. He told me to go with him, and he drove to an office complex off of Highway 99 in Tigard. There was a front reception area, and a door that led to the back office. I thought I was going to see the dope. Instead, a big guy was waiting for us.

His name was Jack, and he took me into the back office and sat me down on a chair, held me down and took out a gun. The floor was covered with a tarp. I knew I was in trouble. Jack knocked me off the chair a couple of times while Joseph did the talking, explaining the severity of what had happened.

"You sent me down there, gave me money, and what you did was disrespectful," he admonished. "Why'd you send me down there if you didn't have the money?"

"You were gone a week," I said. "I figured you ripped me off. It wouldn't be the first time."

He brought up the issue of the cocaine, blaming me for not having the money to pay for it.

I reminded him that it was more a misunderstanding. I'd asked if he could get it. I didn't tell him to get it for me.

"When I put things in motions, people listen," he said. He wanted to teach me to live up to my end of the bargain.

I said, "Just give me half of it," but he wouldn't listen. It was all or nothing.

I made some phone calls from the chair, trying to round up the money, and I was successful. Once Joseph knew I had the money on the way, the big guy got friendlier and left. Joseph then went on to explain to me that this is how the business worked.

"If you're ever in a situation like this, Jack is a resource we can all use," he said. "We're a team."

Some team. Some life.

Looking back

Everybody in the world of drugs has their own interests, and addiction and money are more powerful than friendship. People will be your friends until something comes along that serves them better. And something better will always come along. Joseph always claimed he was trying to show me how the business worked, that he was trying to teach me a lesson. Even if he did believe that—and I doubt it—the only things he cared about were the money and himself.

CHAPTER SIXTEEN
BACK TO BUSINESS

What I have always valued most in our friendship is a much more subtle expression of your fearlessness: your complete openness and your complete devotion. In these two, you have never hesitated. I admire that above all else.

—J.D., a longtime friend

Joseph and I formed a business relationship and later became friends, and I visited the office numerous times after that. I looked at it as a learning experience. That's how out of it I was. Joseph had brought in a thug to teach me a lesson, and I looked at it as bonding.

I liked hearing about Joseph's experiences, but I didn't learn from his mistakes. The successful drug dealers are the ones who don't make exceptions, who do things the same way every time and don't deviate from the plan just because a friend wants a better deal.

Joseph and I had been working together for a couple of months, selling a lot of drugs. I'd come pick up drugs at all hours at his CPA office. But, the only business he did out of that office was drugs. That's why he always wanted me to be painting or doing something other than dealing, to create a respectable front. However, I was more about the drugs and getting high than working, so he lived his fantasy, and I lived mine.

Most of the successful drug dealers he knew were successful business people who were selling drugs to make huge income. Not all of them were addicts. The best drug dealers and the most ruthless are the ones who aren't using. It's all about the money to them.

San Francisco

Joseph had kind of hinted that one day, he'd tell me the whole story about San Francisco and the mysterious amber glass he manufactured. When he came over one day, I was ready for it. Joseph brought out this whole chart about drugs and chemicals for me and explained his version of manufacturing.

When I was growing up, if my dad told me something was the truth, I didn't question it; my dad saying it made it true in my eyes. If you don't know the truth, when someone draws stuff down on a piece of paper the way Joseph did, and shows you charts and graphs, you're going to believe what he's saying. I did. It doesn't necessarily have to be the truth; it just has to sound like the truth.

"So," I said. "If all of this is true, and you were making all that money selling amber glass, what are you doing living with your parents? Why aren't you still in San Francisco?"

That's where I came in. "Once we start making amber glass, you can go back and take over San Francisco," he explained. He couldn't go back himself, and the reason was part of what he'd been promising to tell me. According to him, he was manufacturing amber glass and had an entire drug network, and on a Friday, the FBI had come in and arrested him. Instead of booking him and putting him in jail—according to Joseph—they threw him in a basement of a house and fed him bread and water for months. No one knew where he was, and they then arrested the top eight people in his organization.

The point, he said, was to make it look as if he had snitched on everyone else. He wasn't in jail, not in San Francisco. So everyone jumped to the conclusion that Joseph turned on his top eight people to get himself out of trouble. One day, they came down to the basement, and they kicked him out onto the streets. He went to the first person he knew. You can imagine what he must have looked like after six months. The person to whom he went seeking help accused him of ratting on everyone.

He was beaten up numerous times, and no one would believe his story. That's why he came to Portland. He had no place else to go. As he talked, I tried to decide if I should believe his story. First of all, I hadn't seen the amber glass yet. I also didn't really believe the FBI story. *Why would they do that?* I wondered.

But, it could have been true. People in prison have almost as much power as they do when they're out. Locking him up wouldn't have accomplished much. By putting Joseph in the basement and discrediting him as a snitch and a liar, they'd effectively stopped him. I'm not saying it did happen that way, but it could've.

Manufacturing/dealing amber glass

Two or three weeks later, a driver delivered my pounds of crank in plastic zip lock bags inside a cooler with ice. I took the cooler to Heather's, a redhead I'd always had a crush on. When I got there, I discovered that one of the pounds was wet because the bag was not sealed. I had a pound of wet crank, and that was not good. I didn't have a clue what to do to it. I didn't want to sound like an idiot, so I put it in Heather's freezer. I was hoping it would harden, but that didn't fix it. I put it on a bowl over a light. Crank is a little more unstable than crystal. As it evaporated for a few hours, I finally called Joseph.

"Don't do anything else," he said. "I'll be right down there." Once he arrived, he put the crank in his briefcase and left. I was pretty spun and knew that there was no way I was going to make it to my apartment. Fortunately, Mack's girlfriend lived down the road. I crashed at her place and yet one more time never made it to meet Dee.

The next day, I went over to the office, and even after watching him manufacture, I had no idea how Joseph did what he did. He started out with clear liquid in a container and said we need to keep it there for the whole process to take place. At the end of the thirty days, we had a big chunk of amber glass at the bottom, and at the top, there was a red liquid, which we poured off.

The effects of smoking amber glass are much more intense than if you snort it. I'd smoked a little bit of crystal at that time, but Joseph told me that if I ever smoked the amber glass, he'd cut me off and never give me anything else. It was much more addictive that way, he explained. I'm not sure if he was really concerned about how addicted I got, or if he was being controlling, but I was amazed by the sight of the amber glass.

Regular crystal is kind of hard, but it's not the strong structure of glass. Joseph got a laser light, shined it into the amber glass and showed me how the light was caught in a prism so that I could see how pure it was. His plan was for me to go out and sell this stuff for the outrageous price that he sold it for in San Francisco. I always liked ecstasy and was always looking for a good connection for that, so Joseph used my attraction to try to entice me to sell amber glass in San Francisco, where ecstasy was rampant. According to him, the person who wanted to buy the amber glass was a good source for ecstasy.

"If you go down there with the amber glass," he told me, "you'll get the ecstasy."

I never went down there, so I never found out if it was the truth or just another one of Joseph's lies.

From the start there were some problems with his strategy. Sure, I could show off the beautiful glass to someone with the laser light, and I could demonstrate how difficult it was to chop. But the nuts and bolts, when we got down to it, was the result. Amber glass was not like regular crystal.

The amber glass appealed to businesspeople who had to go to work in the morning and wanted the purest, cleanest stuff. But the people I was dealing to were drug dealers, addicts and partiers. There was no real market for amber glass in Portland. The price of regular crank was sixteen hundred an ounce, and Joseph wanted from three thousand, five hundred to five thousand dollars an ounce for amber glass. The addicts couldn't afford it, the partiers didn't need it and the dealers couldn't profit from it.

People didn't believe the stories about his past or in the power of amber glass. It would be one thing if I'd started with Joseph from the outset. Then I could have filtered in the glass into the population in small stashes to build up word of mouth about our new product, instead of hitting the buyers with the full amount before they'd had a chance to sample it.

I was sold on his plan, but I had to sell everybody else on the idea. Someone like Brody was used to paying a certain price for drugs, so he worked with me only because we were friends. It was tough for me to get Brody to buy into amber glass or working with Joseph. I was limited by what Joseph told me. Although my product was better, why would Hank want to go from paying what he was to what Joseph was asking?

But the biggest problem was that there wasn't an endless supply. There were times when I had three or four pounds. But other times, I had nothing to sell. Part of it was Joseph's fault because he needed to get his volume going. That's the only reason he agreed to selling Hank pounds for eight thousand dollars. Still, it was difficult for him to say it was okay to sell Hank pounds for that but stick to set pricing for everyone else.

Brody was the one who gave me my start, so I felt I should be giving him the best deal possible. We ended up creating too many drug dealers because of the availability. People lost their jobs. It kind of got out of control for a while. In drugs, people always wanted to get a better deal. They thought the more they sold, the better deal they should get.

As I said, Joseph insisted on set pricing. The business had been around for years, he said, and there was only one way that it worked. When I started selling pounds to Hank for five hundred to a thousand dollars more than I got them for, I just ruined the whole operation. In my head, I was thinking,

More volume. If I sold a pound to Hank, then we could move ten pounds a week instead of five. By doing that, I broke the whole structure.

Brody would want an ounce and ask for the best deal possible. So I'd give the ounce to him for six hundred dollars. In my head, I was thinking if I'd give it to Brody for six hundred, and he listened and did what I told him, he could come back with twelve hundred—Joseph's set pricing. But, by my dropping the price, Brody would come back with only one hundred dollars and expect more product at six hundred. That put us five hundred dollars short of our goal—which was very bad.

Every time a drug sale was made, Joseph said, the money should have doubled, and the money should have flowed to the top. If the top person didn't have any money, then nobody was going to have any drugs. If the drugs were sold too cheap, there would be fewer to sell. I didn't maximize the amount of money that should have been generated by a certain volume. I flooded the market. End users who were working at jobs and just using on the weekend became dealers because they could get it so cheaply. It created more drug addicts, more dealers and less money. Joseph told me that that the market would dry up and blow away if I allowed that to take place—and that's actually what happened.

While my dealing business was suffering its ups and mostly downs, Dee and I were doing the same. I continued my old habits of promising to meet her and then showing up late or not at all, and she wasn't shy about letting me know how she felt about it. Impulsively, I bought a hundred roses, put them in a box and left them on her doorstep. The roses improved our relationship, but not for long.

Looking back

Money was power to me back then. When I had ten thousand to twenty thousand dollars in my pocket, I thought I was something special. I've learned since then that all the money did was give me a false sense of security and false sense of worth. Drug money is not like a paycheck received from a regular job. It's easy come, easy go. The minute you take it out of your pocket, it can be taken from you, and so can anything else—including your life.

CHAPTER SEVENTEEN
HIGH ROLLING

I've seen him in his good and in his bad, and he was always the same person inside. The drug haze really changes people. I finally sucked it up and got my life together. He and I were the lucky ones. We got out.
— Artie, a longtime friend

I'd just turned twenty-one in 1995, and our favorite DJs, Sasha and Digweed—the ones I'd seen in Portland—were going to be in San Francisco. Everybody we partied with got together and decided to go down to San Francisco. Joseph was in Los Angeles, and it was July 2. I was a little spun out because all of the drugs and partying I'd been doing.

Joseph wanted to pick up four or five pounds of meth, and I was trying to round up as much money as possible to send down to him. He called me in the morning even though I'd been partying all night long, telling jokes, doing what had become my stand-up routine. That was one of the reasons I liked selling drugs. Everywhere I went was like a new stage. New people to gather around and new girls to meet.

But then, all I could think about was the twelve thousand dollars in my hand, ten thousand of which I needed to send down to Joseph. Weighing money was a shortcut for me. Counting out ten thousand dollars in twenties can take a long time. But I learned from Hank that every bill weighs a gram. So, as long as they were the same denomination, I could just weigh it and see how much money I had. We still counted the bills, but the scales were a way of verifying and saving time.

Instead of using Western Union for large quantities of money, I usually sent it Delta Dash through the Delta airlines. It was Joseph's suggestion, and one I actually followed. With a box I lined in carbon paper, I'd put the money inside, cover it with more carbon paper and take it to the airport. On this day, thanks to my partying the night before, I wasn't in any condition to try to get it out to the airport, so I sent my roommate, Daniel. I got the package all ready for him and gave him the instructions, and then I continued to party.

The next day was July 3, and I had another big chunk of money that I needed to send down to Joseph. That morning I was at Dee's apartment with Trey, in even worse shape than I'd been the day before. After I missed two shipment flights, I had Trey take care of it for me. That meant that Joseph had all of the money that I needed to send him.

I was waiting for him to come back from Los Angeles with this big shipment, so that I could distribute it before we drove down to San Francisco. The party was at the Sound Factory. The morning of the fourth rolled around, and everyone who was going had already left. Somebody had stolen a van and switched license plates on it, and about twelve of them loaded into the van and caravanned with a few other vehicles. Several of my friends offered me a ride, but I had no choice. I needed to wait in Oregon.

About six people in my group were waiting with me, and ever the pleaser, I promised them that we'd get to San Francisco one way or the other. About three p.m., Joseph called and was still stuck in Los Angeles. I was calling commercial airlines to try to schedule a flight for my friends and me to San Francisco. The later it got, the more it looked like we weren't going to make it down there to party. All of the people I'd asked to stay were upset with me. The people I needed to get the drugs to weren't so happy either.

Joseph decided that he was going to charter a Learjet in Los Angeles and fly to Portland. I knew that we'd have about six seats. I wanted Dee to go, along with three girls she knew. Frank, a younger guy, who was part of our group, also wanted to go. Craig was at my house and was whining that he wanted to come along. I had to tell him no. He owed me money, and I told him I needed him to take care of business for me. I gave him some drugs to sell and some business to do.

At about ten p.m., when everyone was glum and thinking that we'd missed the party, I told my buddies and Dee that we were heading for the airport. When Joseph landed, I met him and grabbed the drugs that he had. Then I ran up the street, met some of my dealers and distributed the drugs. Then I got on the jet with my friends, and we took off. As we did so, we all took a couple of hits of ecstasy. We were in San Francisco almost before we started getting high.

It was already after midnight. We got to the party, went inside, and everybody wanted to know how we got there.

"Oh, we took a Learjet," I said.

"No way."

It was a good party, with one of the best laser light shows I'd seen at that time. It was one of the up sides of my life then, one of the fun times I'd like to talk about when I'd remember those times later.

Mack—everyone needs one

Mack was Brody's number-one. He was a storyteller, one of those guys who would jump into someone else's story, finish it and top it off by saying, "I was there." The first time it happened, I was telling the story about the motorcycle with Hank. Bobby J. stepped in, took over the story, finished it off as well as I could have and said, "I was there. I just happened to be coming around the corner when it was happening." My story happened to be true, but I could and did exaggerate many of my tales, and he always enhanced them in the same manner.

Looking back

At this time in my life, I still thought people were good. I thought they were honest and trustworthy. If I were nice to them, they'd be nice in return, I thought. I didn't realize that when drugs enter the scene, values go out the window. No one is immune, and neither was I.

CHAPTER EIGHTEEN
THE SNOWBALL EFFECT

*I'm not going to lie. We had good times. But we also had bad times,
and the bad outweighed the good. Other than Mikael, I'd never want
to see any of those people again. He was my friend, but with the rest of
them, it was all about the drugs.*
—Artie, a longtime friend

That night in San Francisco, we partied until about seven the next morning. We
partied there for a couple of days. Dee and I flew back on a commercial flight.

Everybody gets in trouble eventually. There are things you can do to
slow down the snowball effect, but ultimately, it gets away from you, and
there's nothing you can do to stop it. With every business, there needs to be
a business plan, and if you deviate from that, you fail.

Craig was a constant drain. He would always come back with not only an
excuse, but a plan to make back the money he'd lost. And every time there was a
plan, it involved an investment on my part. So where did I cut my ties? At five
grand? At ten? Everybody has to get lucky one time, I reasoned. Craig never did.

One day, a police officer pulled me over on my motorcycle, with dope and
money on me. I figured if I just pulled over, they wouldn't look in my bag, while
if I tried to get away, they probably would chase me down, check out everything
and arrest me. I had no license or insurance, so they had to tow my bike.

The tow truck driver let me off at the bottom of the complex. The
officer followed me and said it wasn't the address I'd given him. I explained
that the address I'd given was my parents' and that I moved around a lot.

Hank would be there any moment, I knew. I hurried inside to call him before he encountered the officer. Too late. As I went into my apartment, I heard a motorcycle with sirens behind it screaming. They went to the top of the complex, and it was silent. Then, the sirens went on again.

Later I learned that after the chase to the top of complex, Hank shut his lights off. The police did the same. When Hank saw the officer behind him, he flipped on his lights and took off. The police tried to block the road, but by the time Hank got to the road, he was far ahead of them. Finally, they blocked it on the other side of the freeway.

When he saw the roadblock, Hank swung back around toward the police. He shot down the off ramp into traffic at a hundred and forty miles an hour and got away. It was dangerous, but it was also second nature for him. It wasn't the first time he'd run away from the cops.

A few weeks later, he was parked in his Ford Expedition at Crown Point. In the same way I was Joseph's number-one, Hank had Victor as his. But Victor was from a different crowd than I was used to. So was Hank, which was why he always bought all the toys. He'd never had any as a kid, and working as a drug dealer gave him an opportunity to buy all of the grown-up toys he wanted.

Victor and Hank were smoking crank, and of course, there were guns in the car. Hank loved guns. Any time he could get his hands on a new one, he had to have it. He had a grenade launcher and everything else you could imagine, and even though he didn't have a driver's license, he drove around with his guns.

They were out in the middle of nowhere, and a police officer drove up. He asked for his ID, and Hank gave it to him. When the officer went to run it, Hank took off. They were chasing him around the winding roads, and Hank finally drove the truck into a field and ran. Victor didn't, so he got arrested. That was the start of Hank's decline. Now the cops had his name, and they were actively looking for him. Anytime you have guns and drugs together, it's a major deal, and when the cops searched his vehicle, they found both.

Hank was on the run. He started getting really paranoid. After the incident with the Expedition, he got farther and farther away. Ultimately he went on a road trip with his girlfriend, turned over his operation to another guy and left town owing me about twenty grand.

Oh, Canada

Miles was a regular customer, one of my dealers, good for an ounce or two every day. He paid a higher price than Brody or some of the others. He was on a front basis, where I fronted him the dope, and he sold it. He always paid me. A lot of the other people didn't have a home base and moved around a lot. Not Miles. His life consisted of staying in his home, selling drugs to people. That was his little world.

He was into the rave scene, and he knew some DJs from Canada who had spun records in Portland. He figured if he could hook these people up in Canada, we could double our money. As I mentioned before, "double your money" was a dream I chased for too many years. When it sounds too good to be true, it usually is. That was the case with Canada.

Joseph wanted to be sure I charged him the right amount. "But most of all, whatever you do, don't let him cross the border," he said. "Make him meet the guy on this side."

In the world of drugs, if you cross state lines, you deal with the FBI, but if you cross the border, it's DEA you're dealing with. Any large cocaine bust usually involves DEA because all coke comes from outside the country.

Miles didn't have a driver's license. Lilly, one of the girls Miles knew, was going to drive. She had a license and insurance. And once I met her and talked to her, I felt comfortable that she was capable and that I probably could trust her. I gave her the same spiel that I did Miles. "Don't go over the border. Don't break the speed limit. Don't do anything stupid." The basic stuff.

Then I wrapped the drugs in duct tape, found a compartment inside the car and hid them in there. Miles and Lilly left around noon. Bellingham, the nearest border city, was about a four-hour drive. Miles was supposed to call when he got there just to let me know that everything was okay.

He didn't call that night. The next day, around five p.m., Lilly called me. Miles hadn't done what I'd asked. The people with whom he was dealing offered him extra money if he'd bring the drugs across the border because they were smart enough to know better than to do it themselves. So, he took the drugs out of where I'd hidden them and tried to cross the border.

When the border patrol started to search the car, Miles freaked out and ran. They detained Lilly and impounded her car. I had to pay to fly her back down to Oregon. She was in tears when I picked her up at the airport.

Her dad called me for weeks after because they couldn't get her car back. "My daughter doesn't do drugs," he said. "If she'd known what was going on, she never would have agreed to it."

Lilly knew what was going on, but parents don't want to know what their kids do.

When I finally got hold of Miles, I was with Trey. I went into his house and said, "Hey, Miles, what's going on?" I wanted him to tell me the story of what happened.

Mikael, Lara, Kelianne and Jeremy 1979

Mikael soccer photo, 1984

Mikael as a baby

Mikael seventh birthday.

Mikael 18 months old

Mikael little league, 1980

Mikael's 16th birhtday party.
What a great group of friends.

Family, 1990 Jeremy, Mikael, Mom, Dad,
Lara, Kelianne

Family 1982

Best Friends

Hood to Coast 106 mile running
relay, Mt. Hood to Oregon Coast.

Cascade Run-off, Portland,
Oregon 15k 13 years old.

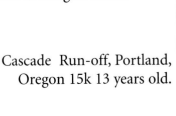

1991 State 400 meter relay team. David, Mikael, Coach Bell, Troy and Carey.

Mikael crossing the finish line anchoring the 4 x 400 meter relay.

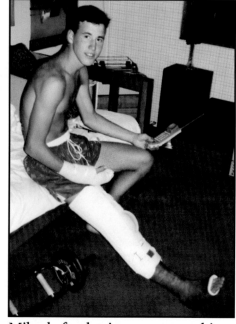

Mikael after having surgery on his knee and hand with a broken ankle.

Modeling photos before drug use

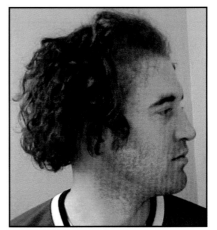

Final arrest Nov. 2, 2000, after
eight years of drug use.

Pearce and Mikaila 2007

Mikaila Olivia 18 weeks old

Mikael and Amanda engagement
photo Jan. 2005

800 meter book cover on the back of the trailer.

Mikael and Coach Yarnell at the start of the
12,000 mile bike ride

Truck and Trailer leaving on 12,000 mile bike ride

Crowd waving goodbye: The crowd waiving goodbye as Mikael leaves on 12,000 mile bike ride.

Reader board at Aloha High School when Mikael was leaving on 12,000 mile bike ride

Lilly hadn't wanted me to know that they'd gone across the border. She said originally that they got pulled over, and the car was impounded. Miles didn't want to tell me the truth either. He had glass shelving against the wall. I grabbed the shelving and pulled it down. It hit the coffee table, sending glass everywhere. Then he told me the truth about what had happened.

Lilly had given them Miles' name, so his time was limited. He owed me around eight grand, but he packed up and left. The only way he could pay me was to sell more drugs. But he couldn't stay in his apartment anymore because the police would be there any minute. I lost that money, and I have no idea what happened to Miles.

After that, Lilly went totally downhill.

Remember Pinkie, who slept in a broken-down van in the parking lot of his son's strip joint? You wouldn't think he could get a girl even if he had money, right? But after what happened in Canada, Lilly was living with Pinkie in the van. At first, her dad didn't realize that the problem was her. He wanted to blame Miles or me.

Finally, I said, "Your daughter is not who you think she is. She might be a nice person, but she's addicted to drugs, and she knew what she was doing when she went up there."

Her parents hired a detective, tracked her down and tried to do an intervention. They took her forcefully from Pinkie's van, which was probably the best thing they could have done. Everyone needs a wake-up call. I hope · that was hers. I'm sure that Lilly never planned on living in a van with a fifty-year-old man who'd been an addict since Vietnam. That was Lilly's snowball. It's addiction, and it's what poor choices lead to.

Time to collect

When we got back from San Francisco, we went to a rave. Lance, one of my dealers, had owed me money, and it was getting to a point where I had to do something. He arrived at the rave in a Corvette convertible. I told Trey to grab him and put him in Brody's stolen van so that I could talk to him. It wasn't like me to do that, but it had built to a level that I had to do something. Seeing that car was what did it; I'd had enough.

I was waiting in the van when Trey and some other guys brought Lance in. He gave me a hard-luck story. I asked about the Corvette, and he said it was partial payment for a drug deal. So I took the keys and told him it could be partial payment for the ten thousand dollars he owed me. After driving it that night, I realized that the car was too high-profile for me. Lance needed transportation to get back to Seattle to finish a deal. Trey let him take his car, and Trey held onto the Corvette. Lance came back with partial payment and two hundred fifty vials of what he called "liquid ecstasy." I took two vials of it, and a half hour after I'd left Dee's on my motorcycle, I was so high that I had to park the bike. I knew it wasn't ecstasy.

Trey picked me up, and he was in no shape to drive either. Every time he put his foot on the accelerator, it gave him the chills, so I ended up driving the Corvette back to Dee's place. We didn't want the high to stop, so we kept doing vials of the liquid. The next morning, Austin's brother came over to buy some drugs. He was about nineteen, and I figured he'd do what I asked. So I said, "I want you to go pick up my motorcycle and bring it back to Dee's apartment by eight in the morning. If you do, I'll get you more drugs."

I never missed a summer softball game, and I had one scheduled that night. By noon, Austin's brother still hadn't returned. When I called Austin, he said that he didn't know where he was. I finally drove the Corvette to the game. When I was high, I didn't care about the motorcycle, but after the softball game, I wanted it. I finally tracked him down at Austin's. My bike was in the driveway, wrecked. Austin's brother claimed it had just toppled over and that he was going to get it fixed as soon as he had the money. The same old story. I asked him to make sure he delivered the bike to Dee's. Instead, he wrecked it again. I finally sold it to someone who was going to rebuild it. The motorcycle phase of my life was over.

I'd been pulled over four times on it. Two of those times I probably had a pound or more of meth and ten to fifteen thousand dollars in cash on me, along with scales and baggies. The first time, I got towed for no insurance. The other times, all they did was give me a ticket for driving without a license and tell me to get someone else to drive it. That didn't bother me. I just waited until they left.

Most people who ride motorcycles don't pull over; they just outrun the cops. I knew that I wasn't a very good motorcycle rider, compared to Hank. If I tried to run and got caught, they'd probably search in the bike bag. But my stopping made me look as if I had nothing to hide. Furthermore, I looked clean-cut and calm—not a stereotypical drug dealer—and I always treated the police officers with respect. I didn't have much fear of getting caught because I always seemed to get out of trouble as fast as I got into it. And in the back of my mind was the thought that I could always run if I had to.

I did some research and realized that the liquid was actually ketamine, a general dissociative anesthetic. The effects were similar to ecstasy but it almost makes you feel like you're in a cartoon. Since no one knew what ketamine was, we marketed it as liquid ecstasy so that we could get more money for it.

Looking back

It's difficult to imagine how rapidly somebody's life can change once they get caught up in addiction. You may not see it, but everyone around you can. Different people spiral down at a different rate. Lilly went from decent to living in a van within two weeks of one event. She got no second chance. I was getting second chance after second chance, and I should have known that my chances were going to run out too.

CHAPTER NINETEEN
DODGING BULLETS

"It's all good, brother."
—Drug jargon used by someone who owes money

Trey always felt that I owed him for the connection with Hank, and he wasn't shy about asking for favors. If the power at the bar was going to be turned off, I'd have to lend him the money to pay for it. One of his goals was to learn to manufacture, and he was working with his dad Pinkie's biker friends to learn how. He wanted me to ask Joseph if he could get the chemicals from Mexico. At this time, no one had met Joseph. I got the chemicals for Trey and put them in the back of his car.

Trey owed a small amount of money to Brody's girlfriend, Ren. As people did in our line of work, Brody decided he was going to collect by stealing Trey's car. He was like that. He wouldn't get in your face, but he'd steal your car.

We were at Dee's apartment, where I was living. I made a few calls and found out he was hiding out at the house of Max and his stripper girlfriend, Bunny. We took Dee's car there to confront Brody. They said he wasn't there, and I got aggressive. I went into the garage where they had a dance floor, turntables, records and a couch Brody was sitting on. With a rush, I jumped Brody, and had to be pulled off of him. He shot out the back door and took off. With Trey driving Dee's car, we pulled in behind him. I grabbed Trey's gun, cocked it and tried to fire it, but nothing happened.

"Take the safety off," Trey yelled.

I did, but nothing happened. Just like the movies, I was hanging out the window, aiming for the tires. Brody got away, and Trey and I went back to his house. The bullet was jammed in the chamber.

I had to call Joseph and let him know that the chemicals were stolen. He demanded Brody's phone number. When Joseph called him, he was nice and offered to return them. This was what Brody had always wanted, an opportunity to get connected to Joseph.

Joseph got the chemicals back, and I got them from him. I was supposed to meet the bikers just outside of town. They had me follow them over the train tracks out in the middle of nowhere. In my mind, I already knew I was getting ripped off. That was confirmed when I got out of the car.

One of them pulled a gun and said, "We're taking the chemicals."

I was probably more pissed off than scared. I gave up the chemicals and drove back to Trey's bar. He tried to convince me that he didn't have anything to do with what they'd done, but I'm sure that he did. They were his father's friends.

Joseph started losing faith in me. At the beginning, I was his number-one. He didn't deal with anyone else, and no one knew who he was. That was the way he wanted it. At first, he was extremely isolated. I was going out, preaching about his new drugs, but I didn't say where I was getting the information because of Joseph's need to stay anonymous. It's tough to preach something when you can't reveal the source.

The great almost-shootout at the stripper bar

When you owe money in the drug business, you usually owe a lot of people. That night, a guy from the biker group came into the bar demanding to see Trey. Trey and I were in the office when he pushed the door in. The guy demanded his money; Trey made excuses. I wanted to get out of the middle of it, so I opened the outside office door, grabbed my bike bag and kind of backed out. While they were still arguing, I got on my motorcycle.

At the same time, Hank and Santos showed up on their motorcycles and proceeded to go for the guy, who Trey was pushing outside the office door. There were three of them and one of him, but then he grabbed Trey's gun off the desk organizer and pointed it straight at me.

Hank and Santos pulled out their guns and ducked between parked cars, and Trey shut himself inside the office. So it was the guy with the gun and me.

I tried to explain to him that I didn't have anything to do with the money that Trey owed him, and he demanded that I pay Trey's debt. Hank and Santos were screaming, "Get out of the way," probably because they wanted to shoot the guy. I eventually got behind the pickup where Santos was, and the guy just put the gun in his jeans and left.

I then had to tell Joseph what had happened and try to make that up to him. At that point, I didn't have a lot of money. I was owed about thirty-five thousand dollars, and I owed Joseph about ten thousand. All of my profit was going to pay him back. Now that Joseph was hooking Brody up directly, I was cut out of that.

Brody continued to drive the stolen van he'd taken to San Francisco. He dealt drugs out of it. It had a different license plate in front than in the back. Because of what had happened in the past, he probably felt like he had a get-out-of-jail-free card. In a way, he did. When you start working with the police, that's what happens. Anytime you get busted, you simply offer the name of somebody higher than you.

Brody was finally arrested after he moved to Hood River with Ren. They got pulled over in the van, and when the cops ran the plates, they discovered it was stolen. After their arrest, Joseph got an attorney for them. Brody used Joseph as his get-out-of-jail-free card. After getting out of jail, Brody continued working for Joseph, but while doing so, he began gathering information for the police.

Brody cared only about Brody. When I worked for Joseph, I cared about the business, and I tried to protect him. Joseph was also caught up in the snowball. Although he tried to make amber glass numerous times, something always went wrong. The people he thought he could trust were the ones he shouldn't have trusted. His life was spiraling downward, as was my own.

The same group of people who went to San Francisco planned to take the train to a party in Seattle. Joe was going with us. He was one of the weekend partiers I'd met at Panorama. He was older, about six foot four, two hundred ten pounds, athletic. He just kind of appeared at an after-hours one night. Dee had known him because Carter had sold him ecstasy in the past. He was against speed, though, and didn't like his girlfriend, Faith, hanging out with Dee and all of the other dancer girls because he was afraid she'd want to be a dancer too. She already looked like one. With her blonde hair, fake boobs, rebellious attitude and willingness to show her body at every opportunity, she was a dancer just waiting to happen.

It was a Friday night, and I was still working with Joseph, even though I owed him money. I went to meet him in downtown Portland and picked up some drugs. With my motorcycle wrecked and sold, I'd bought a silver BMW and was driving that.

As I was leaving, another driver and I turned onto the freeway against a red light with a "no turn on red" sign. A group of city police officers were hidden around the corner. The guy ahead of me got pulled over; they also flagged me down. I had a bag of marijuana and drugs on the seat next to me. I lifted my leg up and kicked the drugs off the seat, then slid them under the passenger seat. When the officer came to the window, I told him that I didn't have a license but that I did have insurance. I gave him an ID, and he said I had a warrant for my arrest for nonpayment of a traffic ticket. I was outside the car; drugs were in the car, and I was certain the cops would find them. They called a tow truck driver, and the officer got in my car. I was sure he'd smell the marijuana. He pulled the car forward, got back out, and the tow truck started hooking it up. I was shocked he didn't discover the drugs.

When I got to jail, I asked if I could pay my five-hundred-dollar bail so I could get released. A guard said I had to wait to get shipped to a second jail before I could get out. A second guard helped me out, and I was released around two-thirty a.m. A friend of mine picked me up and then we had to go to the tow yard to get the drugs out of the car. With the tow yard guy at my back, I managed to get the drugs, put them under my shirt and walk out. I got the car back later.

We met at the train station at six a.m. There were about eighteen of us, and we took over one of the train cars. It was one of the first times that I remember doing nitrous oxide—laughing gas. It's either taken from a tank, in a balloon, or as whippets—small metallic cartridges of nitrous oxide intended for home use in whipped cream charging bottles. After opening the whippet, I could release the gas into the balloon.

When Craig showed up at the station, he had the usual ring of crank around his nose. As you can guess, none of the other passengers were excited about sharing the car with us. We had it all to ourselves.

We got to Seattle around noon. Brody and Ren showed up. Joe had started painting with my dad and me, and we'd become better friends. He and I bought matching black Carharts overalls, white t-shirts, white gloves and white Kangols—British sniper caps with the bills turned behind. When we were getting on the elevator heading to the rave, I looked at Joe, who was all muscles. He was wearing his t-shirt and overalls and mine were wearing me. I felt really stupid.

While we were on the elevator, somebody said something about Faith's body because she was wearing a skimpy shirt.

"Hey, Faith, show them your boobs," Joe said, and she did with no hesitation.

I got too high at the party and by the second half, I was just lying on Dee, watching people. We left to go back to the hotel, and out of the blue, I said, "I ain't afraid of no ghosts."

We parked the car and walked past a building that had a huge hole in the front window. Once we were in the hotel room, we started doing nitrous. Craig came in, and I was still tripping on the broken window I'd seen. I almost felt as if the window wasn't broken. When he said that he saw it, he asked if we'd broken it. I said no, but that we'd gone inside and stolen a bunch of computers.

His first reaction was that we shouldn't have done it. But in the same breath, he said, "Oh, I've got someone I can sell them to."

That's how we all kind of thought. We were all trying to make money so that we could get more drugs.

Looking back

There's no logic in addiction. Everybody jumps to conclusions, and everybody reacts without thinking about the consequences. I was willing to jump Brody, to try to shoot out the tires of the car he was driving, and two weeks later, was partying with him in Seattle as if nothing had ever happened. As ridiculous as that sounds, it was just another day in the life.

CHAPTER TWENTY
FEELING INVINCIBLE

I could stay clean if I could just get out of town.
—Bobby J.

A week or two after the party, Joe offered to drive Lance back to Seattle to get drugs from his connection there. Rumor has it that while they were up there, Joe was high on ecstasy, and got into a sexual situation with a man pretending to be a woman. At the same time he was in Seattle, Faith begged Dee to help her get a dancing job, so Dee got Faith a shift at Jodi's. Everybody was afraid about what Joe would do when he found out. He'd given Faith a ring and asked her to marry him because he felt it was the only way to keep control of her. He'd made it clear he didn't want her dancing.

When Joe got back, he was a different person, and he was mad at Lance. He was also upset with Faith for dancing and with Dee for arranging it. Of course, once Faith danced, she didn't want to stop. Dancing is like any other addiction—the money, the attention. It's like somebody saying, "Just do speed one time." One time was all it took for Faith. She wasn't going to stop for Joe or anybody else. A week later, she quite publicly fooled around with an acquaintance of Joe's in the parking lot at Jodi's. Joe heard about it, and it was the beginning of the end of their relationship.

Dee had never liked Joe and always felt it was he, and not Brody, who had turned Carter in. Joe was the kind of person who was always trying to make an easy buck. He wouldn't lower himself to being a drug dealer, but he would pull insurance scams and once pushed his car over a cliff to collect the insurance money. I think what happened next was a result of his greed. People like Brody turn people in to save themselves. Others, like Joe, do it for money, because they are vindictive, or both.

I wasn't getting drugs from Joseph the way I had been. Lance had met some Mexicans down in Woodburn who were going to supply us. We went there and met them at a hotel, where we bought a half-pound of crank. Then we drove back in my BMW to the apartment I shared with Dee—the same apartment where Carter had been busted. I didn't have a cell phone at the time, but I had a pager. I told Lance to drop me off at the front of the complex, where there was a pay phone. I made the phone call, arranged to meet someone and went back to the apartment to get Lance. He still had the keys to the car, so he decided to drive.

As we started to turn, a police car turned left onto our street, then flipped a U-turn to get behind us. After we turned left, the police car turned on its lights and pulled us over into a Denny's parking lot. Within seconds, it went from one police car to six. I knew it was more than a routine traffic stop.

On a loudspeaker, they announced, "Driver. Hands out the window. Passenger. Open the door with your right hand. Step out of the vehicle. Hands in the air."

They made Lance kneel and lie down on the ground.

Then it was my turn.

I had to lie face down while an officer shoved his knee into my back and jerked my hands behind me.

For some reason, they thought we had a gun. Whoever turned us in—probably Joe—made the situation sound a lot worse than it really was.

They put us in separate cars, searched the vehicle and found the drugs. We said they weren't ours. They took Lance to jail and me back to the apartment, saying they wanted to search it. I explained that the apartment wasn't mine; it was Dee's.

When you're in trouble, you're always more willing than you should be to give up information. The cops were looking for a black bag, and I don't know how they came up with that. I knew there was no black bag, and I knew there weren't any drugs in Dee's place. I probably could have demanded that they get a search warrant, but I thought I was safe. I let them search, and they found what I had forgotten I had there—my notebook that had all of my clients' names and other incriminating evidence in it. I didn't get arrested that night, but they left me a card and said if I didn't call on Monday, they would arrest me.

What I found out afterward was that someone had been watching the house and had followed us. Undercover officers don't arrest you; they contact regular officers. The car behind us was probably the undercover officer.

I'm convinced that it was Joe who turned Lance in. I doubt that he wanted anyone else to get in trouble, but it never stops with just one person. Joe was upset with Lance, and he didn't care how he got money. Also, Lance wasn't a major player. It was just a coincidence that we went to pick up the drugs in Woodburn. Further, there was no black bag. That's something the one who ratted out Lance made up to get the police interested. After Lance's arrest, Joe was extremely concerned about me. I don't think he wanted me to be involved.

Who done it?

Two schools of thought existed regarding who was responsible for Carter's big ecstasy bust. Some thought Brody, and some thought Joe. Brody's motive would have been getting himself out of trouble for the marijuana raid at his house. Joe's would have been strictly financial—a paid informant. Those are the worst kind, because paid informants can be even more selective than someone who's in trouble.

When you're in trouble, you can't take a month to find someone to turn in. Joe could have turned me in but chose not to, I believe, because of our friendship. Brody wouldn't have turned me in because of my connection. He needed to know that he still had a source for drugs and drug money. That's why it makes sense to me that Brody turned in Carter. Brody wasn't dependent on Carter's ecstasy. He just needed Carter out of the way so that he could take over that huge portion of the market.

Joe, on the other hand, had already proven his greed with his insurance scams. He had no motive for driving Lance to Washington, but the trip offered him an opportunity to gather information for the police.

Although the police officer had told me to call them on Monday, I waited until Tuesday instead. I needed time to think about options and possibilities. I didn't want to be a rat. When I finally made that call, I asked what they wanted and agreed to talk to them. I also said that I wouldn't give them any information on anyone but myself. The problem was that I had nothing to bargain with. If the police demanded information from me about Joseph, I wasn't sure how long I could remain strong or what the consequences would be. Bottom line: no one wants to go to jail, and I was no exception.

Looking back

Because of my past experiences, I felt as though nothing bad could happen to me. I could have pulled the trigger and shot Brody. The bikers could have shot me. Just getting in trouble with Lance could have gotten me in jail for five years. Again, I seemed one step ahead of trouble; I felt invincible.

CHAPTER TWENTY-ONE
FULL SPEED

Det. Jim Lilly was working with the Regional Organized Crime Narcotics Agency (ROCN) and they wanted to take Mikael out of the center for four hours. He's their primary witness in a Federal Drug Case. Det. Lilly advised that he was actively involved in a drug network and they wished they hadn't offered him immunity from the beginning. He apparently was more involved than they originally thought.
—Probation report

As you can see from the above report, the police didn't know how deeply entrenched in the drug business I was. I believe that's because when Brody turned in Joseph, he tried to protect me by downplaying my involvement. Good old Brody. Now, Lance had been busted, and the police, not aware that I was the number-one man, wanted to interview me. I went downtown that day and talked to them and would continue to do so during the next four months.

In the meantime, Joseph—who was unaware of the case that was being built against him—came to the apartment with two other guys. When I owed him money, he owed other people money, and he wanted to collect.

I didn't have much at that time, and he said, "You've got to give me something to show that you're willing to pay back this debt."

I said, "You can take the BMW."

It wasn't a great loss. I often did nitrous when I was driving it, and a few days before, I'd popped both tires and bent the rims when jumping a curb in a parking lot.

The detectives often called me on my cell phone while I was painting houses. I'd meet them around the corner and answer their questions the best

I could without revealing too much. By the way they asked the questions, I knew they had a lot of information, and that their investigation was pretty much locked up. Finally, my luck ran out, and they didn't want to talk anymore. Instead, they demanded that I go to Joseph's with a wire. They said Brody and others had already done it, which didn't surprise me all that much.

The wire was a pager with a microphone in it. I had no choice, but I wasn't sure if I could rat out a friend or not. They prepped me on the questions they wanted me to ask. All the way to Joseph's parents' house, I was hoping he wouldn't be there. I didn't want to turn him in. He was a decent person. I got out of the car that day wishing I could have been strong enough just to do the time.

The officers waited around the corner. Yes, that's the way it happens in real life. The police wait around the corner promising you they'll be right there if there's trouble. I went up by myself and knocked on the door. No one answered it. I can't begin to describe how relieved I felt. Of course there could be a next time, but I didn't want to think about that right then. I was just so grateful for the reprieve.

As it turned out, I never had to repeat that situation again. Brody had brought a network of his dealers to work with Joseph. One of them ended up owing Joseph money—not a good thing. Joseph had always bragged to me about his connections in California, and when people owed me money, he'd offer to bring in the muscle from there to collect. I never wanted that. Violence was never an option for me. It was for Joseph though.

He called in some contacts from the Mexican mafia, who came with hammers and beat up Brody's dealer. I was sickened. This wasn't what the drug business was supposed to be about. It was supposed to be about spontaneous fun, dancing, sex, laughing, money—and lots and lots of admiration. It wasn't supposed to be about friends ordering other friends to be turned into hamburger meat by thugs wielding hammers. I'd always hated violence, and as addicted as I was back then, I was shocked. I felt as if I were playing a part in a movie, and someone had switched the script on me.

Right after Joseph's connections beat up Brody's dealer, Dee and I went to Panorama one night, and someone said Joseph was there. The hammer victim was also there. The only result of that equation had to be more violence.

He grabbed a glass candleholder off a nearby table, came up from behind Joseph and smashed it on the side of Joseph's face. It wasn't just a little cut. It sliced Joseph's face open. The guy ran out. Joseph fell to the floor. The ambulance came, and all I could see, think or smell was blood.

That was the last time I saw Joseph. Brody and his network provided enough evidence for the Regional Organized Crime Narcotics Agency (ROCN) to arrest him. He agreed to a plea bargain and went to federal prison. That was the end for us as friends and business associates.

Everyone in the drug life always says, "If you have to go to prison, do federal time." Federal prisons are more like country clubs; some have golf courses. Most of the federal criminals are drug dealers and white-collar criminals. I consoled myself that at least Joseph was doing federal time.

My life was changing in many ways. Dee and I lost our apartment. As you may recall, it was the second time the police raided the place—first Carter and then me. It was clear to the apartment managers that Dee didn't have the best taste when it came to men and they didn't want us to be there anymore. We lived with her grandparents at their little house until we got another apartment with none other than Joe, who had broken up with Faith—now a full-time dancer.

Joe felt bad because I'd gotten in trouble with Lance, and that might have been the reason he was so willing to let me get a place with him.

Dust Off

My motto was always, "The higher the better," and I was always trying to come up with a different way to accomplish my goals. I was a natural competitor. Nobody could get as high as I could.

One night I was sitting on my couch, and my friend came in and asked if I had ever tried Dust Off.

"No," I replied, intrigued. "What is it?"

"It's what you use to clean the dust out of electronics," he said.

"And it gets you high?" I asked.

He nodded. "Oh, yeah. It's like nitrous but a little more intense."

"Sounds good," I said. "I love nitrous. Bring it on."

"Go easy," he said.

Easy smeazy, I thought. *I can handle anything.* I grabbed the bottle and inhaled about a five-second squirt, then held it in as long as I could. Nitrous builds as you hold it in, but I soon discovered that the Dust Off got more intense after I had blown it out. The second time I went for a ten-second squirt. I held it in again as long as I could.

After I blew it out, the strangest thing happened. I looked around, and the five people in the room with me were all covered with ice. They looked as if they were from the North Pole—like Santa's helpers. I began to speak, but it wasn't English.

"A ving to the vong to ving to the visan," I said.

Everybody looked at me like I was crazy.

Again I said, "A ving to the vong to ving to the visan."

Nobody responded, and I knelt down on the floor. I decided to take one more hit, and when I did, I dropped the bottle. Next thing I knew, I was lying on the ground. Although I could see the people, it was almost like they couldn't see me. *Am I dead?* I thought. I tried to talk but I couldn't. *Are they talking about me?* I wondered. *I think I'm dead. Does anybody realize that I am lying here dead? Do they care?*

It took me a while before I finally snapped out of it and realized I wasn't dead.

"You're right," I said to my friend. "That stuff is a little more intense that nitrous."

Don't fall in love with a stripper

My relationship with Dee was out of control as well. We'd done ecstasy together, but since she didn't use speed, I didn't when I was with her. The first time she did, she became a paranoid and scary person. We were at a party, and somebody had given it to her. She'd been up for twenty-four hours, and she went from one person to another person in about two seconds. One moment we were all listening to music. The next, she was right in my face, accusing me of something I hadn't even done. She didn't even look like herself—angry, crying and evil. She'd go from punching and hitting me to bursting into tears. I'd seen weird behavior with Karen when she was high, but never like this.

Her friends were trying to calm her down, and she insisted that I was cheating on her and didn't love her. It went on for hours, even after we left and got back to our apartment. Trey was there, and he tried to help me calm her down.

"He doesn't love me," she told Trey.

"Maybe we don't know what love is," he said. "Maybe he really does love you."

This continued through the next morning. She wouldn't calm down enough for me to leave, so I had to take her with me to work with my dad. She wouldn't even sit in the van. She insisted on standing right next to me. For three weeks to a month after that, she still drove by, checking me out, still in that paranoid place.

A couple of months later, I came home from work, and she was high on speed with some of her friends. I was furious. "Whoever gave this to her can sit here and babysit her for the next three or four days while she freaks out," I said.

Another time, I walked in the door, and she started punching me in the face. Her girlfriends who'd gotten high with her felt sorry for me, but there was no stopping her. I went in and lay down on the bed. Dee followed me and kicked me in the back of the head with one of her stilettos and split it wide open. She left, and after an hour or so, one of her friends came back to see if I was okay. I ended up going to her place and staying there for three days. No one knew where I'd disappeared to, and I didn't tell.

There were plenty of times I tried to get out of the relationship. I was depressed and shut down, but I couldn't break away. I always said, "Don't fall in love with a stripper," but I couldn't seem to take my own advice. Dancers were almost always all the same breed. They had bad childhoods or were molested or raped. They never danced sober. I've known only two girls who were able to dance and go to school and make something of themselves.

They also had the money to party all night. When you have one as your girlfriend, there's nothing you can promise her or give her that she hasn't been offered five or ten times that night. When Dee would finally come home, she'd say so-and-so came in, gave her a hundred bucks and promised her that he'd take care of her. I knew a lot of dancers, and I could see the same pattern in almost all of them. No matter how good looking they were or how much money they were earning, they all lacked self-esteem.

Looking back

I stayed in the relationship with Karen because I didn't want to hurt her, and now I was doing the same thing with someone who was far more dangerous. After Karen and I broke up, I carried that behavior into all my relationships and all of my business dealings. I wanted to be the good guy everybody liked, and the price I paid for that was my own self-esteem. The lower you get emotionally, the higher you have to get chemically to feel good about yourself.

CHAPTER TWENTY-TWO
JUST GETTING GOOD

The freaks come out at night, and I come out and freak the freaks.
—Mikael Luman, doing stand-up on drugs

Sometimes my friends could handle the way I partied, but someone new to the group would look at me and ask, "Is he all right?" Many times after a night of partying on ecstasy and acid, I craved nitrous. Being as high as I was, I asked, "Who wants to go get some whippets?"

Nobody seemed to volunteer, so I decided that if I wanted whippets, I would have to go get them myself. I was in no shape to drive, so I decided to call on the services of one of my friends to copilot. We got into the car and headed to the closest Cash and Carry. The drugs were attacking the part of my brain that controlled my sense of direction and location. The five-minute trip down the street was turning into quite the adventure and my copilot was no help. He was worse off than I was at that moment.

Thirty minutes into the trip, I decided to pull over and look in the phone book to see if I could find the address. I had been there a number of times, but the streets seemed to be in a different order that day. The phone book was almost as bad. Although I knew that it was in alphabetical order, I couldn't even figure out the alphabet. I finally gave up on the phone book and decided to do a search and rescue routine.

I drove far enough away from the house until I was way past the store. Then I began to drive back, going up and down the streets. I would turn right and go one block. Then I would turn right again and go ten blocks. Turn left and go a block and turn left again and go ten blocks. I continued to zigzag back and forth until I found Cash and Carry. *I'm so smart,* I thought. When you're high, you always think you are smart even when you do something stupid.

I pulled into the store parking lot and checked myself in the rear view mirror. I was foaming at the mouth—absolutely no shape to be going into a store, but I really wanted to get some whippets. I wiped my mouth and entered the store, knowing there was no way I was going to get what I wanted.

"Where are the whippets?" I asked.

The clerk looked up at me as if I were normal. "How many boxes do you need?"

"Four will do it."

"What are you using them for?" the clerk asked.

Oh boy, I thought. "I have a little coffee booth on the other side of town," I said. I wanted to say something like, "To get high with," and pretend to be joking, but it wasn't worth the risk of them not selling them to me. Besides it took me an hour to find the Cash and Carry. How long would it take me to find the one on the other end of town?

I paid for the whippets and headed to the car, where my copilot was anxiously waiting. I wished I had the cracker with me because I would have done some right there to celebrate.

"I can't believe they sold them to me," I said.

After I had the whippets, I had no problem finding my way back. We returned to the house and entered the room where everyone was waiting.

"What took so long?" someone complained.

"I didn't see any of you volunteering to go," I said. "You're lucky we made it back at all."

Nitrous was good by itself but on ecstasy, it was out of this world. People filled the room—four strippers on the bed, the promoter, my copilot and me. The promoter pulled out a vile of phenol nitrate—head cleaner for copy machines.

Since I had scored the whippets, I felt I should be the first to go. I loaded the cracker with the cartridges, blew out all my air and took in all the nitrous. I held the nitrous in as long as I could and handed the cracker to the promoter to fill again. Then, I blew out the nitrous and took a couple of big hits of the phenol nitrate. After the phenol nitrate, I took another huge hit of the nitrous.

What happened next was out of control. There had been times in the past when I had done too much nitrous and had flopped around like a fish all contorted, but nothing like this. I spun on the floor head over heels until I hit the wall. After making contact with the wall, I counter-spun in a forty-five-degree angle until I hit the other wall. I counter-spun again until I was back to my original position. I stood up on my toes with my knees bent and my body crouched, like a squirrel standing up on its hind legs. I looked around and went back into the spin I had done previously. When I returned back to my original position, I looked over at the promoter needing some type of verification that what I thought just happened actually had.

He nodded with extreme satisfaction and said, "It's just getting good."

Not being able to talk yet, I nodded back and agreed. It was just getting good.

The strippers on the bed had a different idea. They looked terror-stricken. Two of them broke into tears, and they all rushed out of the room, freaked out like they'd seen an exorcist. It took a couple of the girls months before they could talk to me without freaking.

It's amazing what your mind can tell your muscle to do when you fry your processor. I woke up the next morning so sore I could barely walk. If somebody didn't believe me when I told the story, I could send them to ask the promoter. After that, when I ran into him out and about—and we always seemed to run into each other after that—he would always look at me, nod, and say, "It's just getting good."

He was usually right. It was fun then, but it's not fun looking back and realizing that the experience that night could have been the last experience of my life.

Up in smoke

I'd first smoked crystal meth back when Karen and I were together, and I'd smoked it with Hank a few times. Although it lasts longer than cocaine, you need more product to get the proper effect. You get more mileage snorting it than smoking it. In the drug culture, it wasn't as acceptable at first, but ultimately, it became popular, and a lot of people were doing it. Now the head shops sell pipes for smoking crystal. Back then we had to make our own.

We used foil. As the crystal melted, it slid on the foil, and the residue smoked. We inhaled the smoke through portable water bongs. "Doing sliders" was what we called it.

Portland State was a popular school for a lot of Asian students, like my friend Dustin, who was from Indonesia. Those students had nice cars and a lot of cash. Although they were enrolled in Portland State, they didn't go to school and used most of the money their parents were sending them to smoke crystal.

They looked at it more as an art form. "Let's smoke crystal and get high." I looked at it as a bridge. "Let's smoke crystal, get high and go *do* something." Their party *was* the smoking crystal. That was enough for them.

Dustin, who was born in this country, looked at it more the way I did. Positive and upbeat, he wore dark glasses and was a laid-back, Fonzie kind of guy. He had been the Asian connection for ice—which was what the Asian dopers called meth—until his connection fell through, so he'd gone through the same type of situation I had. About the same time, he was dumped by his girlfriend, and the only time he ever thought he was cool was when he was high.

I thought he was cool, though, and I enjoyed hanging out with him. His only downfall was his driving ability. He drove in the whole lane and then some, and he made U-turns whenever he felt like it.

His smoking kit consisted of heavy-duty aluminum foil, an elaborate water bong and a small bottle of denatured alcohol that we used with a wick for lighting. Once he entered our group, we all went from snorting to smoking. I was kind of down from everything that had happened with Joseph, and the way Dustin did drugs offered me a change I desperately needed.

Dukes of Hazzard

He and I shared a fondness for nitrous, too, and he usually had a box or two of whippets with him. One night, we left a rave and were on our way to an after-hours at someone's house. It was about five in the morning and just barely getting light. The rest of the group had left about thirty minutes ahead of us, but the two of us had to keep on dancing. Before we got in the car, I asked if he had any whippets. He did, of course. I got them out of the trunk, and as we drove, I put in three cartridges and begin escalating my already over-the-top high.

"Hey, I want some," he said.

"You can't drive sober," I told him, "and you're already high."

He persisted, but I was worried about his driving, not to mention about him. He was my friend, after all, and even high, I cared about my friends. After much back-and-forthing, I gave him just a tiny bit of the nitrous—imagine a quick hiss: *sss*—and took most of it for myself—imagine a long, slow hiss: *sssssssssss ssssssss*. As we turned onto Canyon Lane, I continued the quick-hiss, long-hiss process. Then I realized that we'd almost gone into the ditch on the right-hand side of the road.

Since I didn't want to be dead that day, I mentioned it to him.

"You're right," he said.

Dustin acknowledged his mistake in a sane-sounding voice, but when I looked back at him, he had a blank stare on his face. His body was there, but no more Dustin. The road curved, and we kept going straight, right off a ten-foot drop that landed us underneath the front bumper of a parked minivan.

If Dustin was comatose, you can imagine what I was after all of that nitrous. Everything was in slow motion. His chest went forward, his arms pulled back. Then the seatbelt caught him. He looked like one of those test dummies in a safety commercial. Just then, because I didn't have my seatbelt on, I went head first into the windshield, broke it and fell back inside the car.

I thought Dustin said, "Run," which seemed like a logical thing to do.

I kicked the door open, scrambled up the embankment and went running up the street. A couple taking their morning walk stopped me and asked if I was okay. I told them my friend Dustin had been messing with the car radio, and we got in an accident as a result. They said I must be in shock. I was in shock all right and hoping they didn't ask what drugs we'd been doing to get us in this situation that early in the day.

The couple and I started walking down to where the car had crashed. Fast-thinking as always, Dustin had already pulled the nitrous canisters out and put them in the trunk. By then the minivan couple and their kids were outside— more concerned about the damage to me than the damage to their van.

Dustin went into first-son mode, pacing back and forth, saying how disappointed his father would be when he learned about the accident. The woman who owned the minivan tried to console him. Can you believe that one? The minivan folks were really decent, nice people. Here we'd wrecked their van and awakened them at five in the morning, and they were concerned about us. The husband asked how we got down there. Miraculously, we went through the chain link fence without hitting any of the posts—and between two trees that were so close together that they ripped the passenger- and driver-side mirrors off the car.

The woman was still consoling Dustin when a police car pulled up. Fortunately, the officer had been called to another accident, and left. We moved the car, and Dustin agreed to pay for the minivan damage.

We then walked the rest of the way to the after-hours. That's right. We had totaled a car, damaged a minivan and escaped the police; we were lucky we had walked away with our lives and all we wanted to do was continue the party. That's how far out of control my life was the night of Dustin's so-called accident.

Looking back

Even in a life out of control, there are wake-up calls. The farther you go out of control, the bigger the wake-up call has to be. The accident with Dustin could have been a blessing that scared me into turning my life around. I was so far out of control by then and so used to living without consequences that it seemed like just another crazy occurrence in my life ruled by drugs.

CHAPTER TWENTY-THREE
LIFE ON PROBATION

"I'm not the one with the problem. I can still make it to work."
—Mikael Luman, on probation

Originally, probation was pretty simple. All I had to do was report once a month and pay my fees. My original crime wasn't drug- or alcohol-related, even though I was drunk when I committed it. After Lance and I were pulled over, I was charged with distribution and possession, and everything changed. I still reported monthly, but when I went in, I had to give a UA—urinary analysis. For a drug user, this isn't a welcomed test. Probation is tough for people who are doing what they're not supposed to be doing.

Even before I was charged, my probation officer gave me a fifteen-day sanction at the jail and then the work release center. Right before I left, I had to do another UA. I still tested dirty, which shows how much I was using. Methamphetamines usually stay in the system no more than forty-eight to seventy-two hours. They thought I'd been using inside, and I had to provide documentation to show them that it is possible to test positive for up to thirty days. Of all the excuses I used and all the lies I told, this time I was telling the truth.

Although I knew when I had to report, I couldn't govern my addiction. I tried something called Test Clean, which you drink a couple of hours before.

The catch is that you're not supposed to use drugs twenty-four hours before, so of course I didn't follow the instructions. On more than one occasion, when I'd report to my probation officer, two officers would show up and arrest me for having a dirty UA from the time before. I also drank half a gallon of vinegar and took Goldenseal—all of the mythical cures. Unfortunately the only way to test clean is to be clean, and that wasn't going to happen.

Eventually, I had to go to the day reporting center, where instead of reporting once a month, I might have to go in once or twice a week. I was supposed to report on a Monday afternoon, and I had partied all weekend. The first thing I remember about Monday morning was being in a girl's car in downtown Portland. I had no idea where I was or who the girl was. Then I remembered that I'd left my van at someone's house. She took me to the other side of the river and dropped me off. I knew I was in no shape to report.

I called Bobby J., who let me use his shower and got me into some clean clothes. I tested dirty, of course, but I thought of it as more of a reference sample since it was my first time there.

I needed to come up with a foolproof plan to pass UAs and I thought I had one. My probation officer said one more and I'd go to jail. No one wants to go to jail, but for a drug addict, the fear of jail isn't as strong as the need to use. It was a Friday afternoon, and I went to my parents' house and asked my dad for some urine. At that time, he was an enabler and just did as I requested. It was a three-part plan and I had part one out of the way.

It was another all-weekend party. Craig was with me, and he was supposed to get me out the door around two o'clock p.m., so that I would have enough time to execute the rest of my plan. He finally got me out around three. We were on the east side of town and needed to get to the west side. Not one to pass up a moment to meet new women, on the way, I stopped and changed a tire for two girls and gave them my phone number. When I got back in the car, my hands were covered in grease.

I pulled into the Beaverton pharmacy, went up to the register and asked for a catheter. The pharmacist said there were four different kinds. I ended up with eighteen inches of tubing and a little squeeze bottle. I pulled into a Texaco gas station, went in the bathroom and started putting the tube in. With the squeeze bottle, I tried to fill my bladder with my dad's urine.

At that moment, the door opened, and the Texaco employee was standing there. I slammed the door, locked it, finished filling my bladder, threw the stuff away, washed my hands and got out of there. When I opened the door to leave, the Texaco guy was still standing there.

At the day reporting center, the loser at the front desk said the last UA was at four forty-five, and it was four fifty-two. It gave him pleasure to tell me I'd have to come back the next day. And there I was with my fancy plumbing job.

When I got back in the car, we decided to go back to the party and Craig started driving. But I still had to pee. On our way back, we stopped at a different gas station, so that I could relieve myself. When I tried, nothing came out except for a few extremely painful drops. I got back in the car with Craig and we continued to the party. Once there, as I was walking up the stairs to the front door, without warning, I started wetting my pants. I got an extra set of clothes from a friend and continued to party.

The next day, when I went to the bathroom, there was blood mixed in with the urine. As it turned out, I ended up getting a kidney and a bladder infection and had to go to the hospital. I told the doctor what I did, and he asked if my hands were clean. Then I remembered changing the tire on the girls' car.

The doctor's note got me out of UAs for a while. About this time, I started seeing a counselor. I lied to him about being clean, so he was telling my probation officer that I was doing well. I finally tested dirty again, the counselor found out that I'd been lying to him, and he refused to treat me.

Getting out of town

Faith, Joe's former girlfriend/fiancée, was out of control. Now a stripper, she was using speed and sleeping around, so he packed up and moved to Las Vegas. We needed someone to pay his share of the rent. That's how Lucy, a dancer and porn star, happened to move in with us.

Her appearance was similar to Dee's—exotic and good looking. There was a rumor that she had HIV. Bobby J.'s girlfriend, Brianna, was with Lucy leaving a club one night when they were involved in a serious car accident. From blood tests, it was discovered that she really did have HIV, and she was in big trouble. At the time she moved in, we thought it was a rumor.

Dee was the only one who knew. In order to appear in porno films, one has to pass an HIV test. Because Lucy and Dee resembled each other, Dee took the test in her place. Lucy was a hustler. I would come home from work and find her there with a loser guy who owned a lingerie shop frequented by the strippers. He was married, almost three hundred pounds and nothing like the type of guys Lucy dated. Yet, she'd be giving him a back rub or hugging on him. Sometimes he'd take out six or seven of the stripper girls, paying for their drinks.

In downtown Portland, there seems to be a strip bar on every corner. It has just about the most strip clubs per capita in the United States. I was friends with around twenty strippers from partying. Once I started dating Dee, I didn't even like going inside the strip bars. I'd go in to play video poker, but the rest of it didn't appeal to me. The biggest problem with dancers was their making it to their shifts. That's all the bar owners cared about.

I saw the whole scene as a dead end for the girls. It gave uneducated girls an opportunity to make a large amount of money in a short time. They had no money-management skills and they had to continue to use in order to take their clothes off. There was nowhere to go from there other than prostitution or porn.

Porn star

A well-known porn star was in Portland, dancing at one of the clubs. She and Dee became friends, so when the porn star was in town, she stayed at our place. She wasn't all that cute but had already done four or five huge movies. After she went home, she invited Dee and the other strippers to hang out with her in California. That meant I could be rid of Dee for a week or two, so it was fine with me.

Dee didn't bother to mention that their real reason for going to California was to appear in a porn film herself. A lot of people who are into meth are addicted to porn. Bobby J. was one of them. It was he who asked me if I'd seen the film. Dee and the other girls got a thousand dollars each. The porn star they thought was their friend was really just recruiting for her film. We never heard from her again.

I was upset that Dee would fall for it, and more upset that she didn't tell me what she'd done. But by then, I already wanted out of the relationship, and I didn't make an issue out of it. There was nothing she could say that would make me feel any better.

You don't lose your girl

There's a saying in jail that you don't lose your girl; you just lose your turn. I discovered this first-hand when I was sentenced to thirty days at the work release center. I didn't necessarily want to be with Dee anymore, but I didn't want anyone else to be, either.

I had violated my probation with a dirty UA, and I had to stay at the center, where I was able to leave a maximum of twelve hours a day to go to work. I asked my dad to say that I was painting for him so that I could leave. One morning, I left the work release center at six a.m. and decided to stop by the apartment to check up on Dee—half-hoping I'd find her doing something she shouldn't. The bus dropped me off, and I went inside. A guy was in the bedroom with Dee, both of them dressed, and he was sitting on the edge of the bed.

Her first reaction was to play it down. "That's just my friend. Come on, you remember? He's that guy I keep telling you about." He was a rocker-type dude whose waist was wider than his shoulders. He wore black jeans, boots and a silver-studded buckle.

I ran full speed and tackled him. Dee screamed and tried to pull me off. He went into the other room, and she yelled at me for beating on him. When I left, he was still there.

Just as they say in prison, I'd lost my turn. Unfortunately, I hadn't lost my girl. Dee claimed that nothing happened, and when work release ended, I went back to the apartment because I didn't know what else to do.

Looking back

Probation is only tough when you don't want to change what you're doing wrong. I was always trying to work outside the system because I was in denial and because it was the way I'd always behaved. I blamed the probation officers, blamed the system, blamed the people I thought got me in trouble. I tried to change situations to benefit me when what I needed to change was myself.

CHAPTER TWENTY-FOUR
HIGH ON ACID

I haven't done this since the last time I saw you.
—One of the lies of the so-called recovering addict

It was New Year's, and although I couldn't get out for New Year's Eve, I did get out early the next morning and went to Derrick's, where everyone was still partying. I told Artie that I needed to leave in a couple of hours to paint for my dad and to be sure to get me out of there. We smoked a little meth and went back into the house.

Someone had left a ten-strip of acid on a table, and I put it on my tongue as a joke. Obviously, I didn't want to take ten hits of acid; I was just kidding around. I took it out and set it back on the table. Soon I was entertaining the group, unaware that my system had absorbed the acid. By the time Artie got me out of there, it was the afternoon.

"Boy, that was some good meth," I told him. Then the light bulb went off in my brain: I was high on acid.

If it had just been meth, I could have still worked. I was trying to think of how to explain to my dad that I was high on acid without incriminating my friends. We met him at the Safeway down the street, and he came up and got into the van. Artie didn't want to be involved in it, so he took a walk. I went into a long explanation about how I'd accidentally taken the acid. I must have talked nonstop for thirty minutes.

After I finished, he said, "Well, do you want to go paint?"

"I just told you," I said. "I'm high on acid." He didn't understand that I was in no condition to work. He was also upset that I was doing drugs when I was supposed to be at the work release center.

When I went back to the center, still tripping on acid, all I could do was lie down on my little bunk. One guy in there had sleep apnea, and I had to listen to his start-and-stop snoring all night long.

Smuggling

I got out of the work release center on January 2. I still had to go to court for the charges resulting from the night Lance and I were stopped and the police had asked me to work with them on arresting Joseph. The judge has the ultimate decision regarding whether or not someone does jail time. My grandfather had just died, and I'd gone to court thinking I was going to get probation.

The district attorney said that I'd worked with them and that he recommended a lesser sentence and three years probation. The judge didn't agree. Because of my past history, he sentenced me to thirty days in jail in addition to the probation. Although I wanted to wait until after my grandfather's funeral to serve my sentence, the judge had me handcuffed and taken to jail right then and there. I was, however, given permission to leave to attend the funeral.

When the people in my cell learned that I was getting a day off, they demanded that I bring tobacco back with me. Fortunately, I was able to pass the body cavity search, and my status and treatment in the jail improved.

"I don't like liars, and I don't like thieves."

After Joseph's arrest, when I stopped being the man for the drugs, I needed to continue to use. Sometimes Gavin would give me drugs, and other times he'd charge me. I was the type of dealer who was always out and about. Gavin just wanted to stay in his house all of the time and tweak. He was what we called a "closet shooter." Translation: he shot meth but didn't want anybody to know it.

He was blonde, thirty-five or older, and before he began dealing full time, he had worked for years for his dad, who had a roofing company. Gavin would do anything for money—forge checks, fake IDs—but he didn't have to commit these crimes himself. He used drugs as a way to get other people to do commit them for him.

One of his friends used to say, "I'm going to church." That meant he'd go to the church parking lot, break into cars and search for purses and wallets to steal. These were the kind of people Gavin kept around him, and they did what he asked them to.

One day he gave me a money order that he couldn't cash. He swore to me that it was good and asked me to try to cash it at my bank. I didn't have a bank account, so I had my dad deposit the money order and cash it. It was for about four thousand dollars, but the bank would give my dad only two thousand before it cleared. Gavin was upset with me for not bringing the full amount. He used that as an excuse to burst into a string of complaints about other people with whom he dealt.

"I don't like liars, and I don't like thieves," he blurted out.

Must have been talking about himself.

On Monday, someone from the bank called and told my dad that the money order was no good. Gavin had known the whole time. He'd let me cause a big problem with my dad at the bank knowing that my dad would get stuck making up the amount. And he'd still blown up at me. He kind of paid it back over time in product, but the drugs that he gave me were poor quality. At the time, though, it was all that I could get.

Liars and thieves. My life was full of them, and Gavin was one of the biggest.

There was no way that I could break up with Dee and live in the same place, so I stopped paying the rent. Joe was already gone to Las Vegas. Lucy was already gone. She and Dee had a huge falling out and fistfight. Dee was threatening to tell people that Lucy had HIV because she didn't like the fact that Lucy was having sex with guys. The secret was too big for Dee to keep.

We got an eviction notice, and I told Dee I was moving in with my parents. She moved back with her grandparents. Even after we broke up, she still wanted to be together. I thought we were finished, but Dee was just getting started.

Looking back

In relationships, I always felt that I could fix or help the other person. Instead, I left them worse than I found them. It wasn't my intention, but it's what happened every time. If I knew that I wasn't going to be with Dee forever, I shouldn't have been with her two weeks. How can a drug addict, drug dealer, liar and thief be able to improve anyone's life? I couldn't stand up for Dee, I couldn't stand up for Karen, I couldn't stand up for any of my women because I couldn't stand up for myself and my values.

CHAPTER TWENTY-FIVE
PARTY PAD

It's all about the music.
—Bobby J., rationalizing his addiction

When I broke up with Dee, my dad helped me rent a house in a nice neighborhood in Beaverton. It had a hot tub and glass windows overlooking a basketball court.

When Mack walked in, he said, "Oh, yeah. I see sex all over this place."

I lived there with Bobby J., Artie and DJ Jazz. Brianna, Bobby J.'s girlfriend, moved in with us after she got out of the hospital following the wreck with Lucy.

There were times when I'd be out partying with a different girl, and somehow Dee would find out, track me down, hit me in the face and threaten to kick the girl's ass. Portland is small, and the strippers all talk. If I was at one place, ten minutes later, so was Dee.

I started seeing Leanne, a sweet girl and manager at a Starbucks. A blonde, she used ecstasy on the weekends and didn't use speed. To that point, she was probably the most decent woman I'd been with.

She had just left a long-term relationship and wasn't sure she wanted to get involved with me. How could she resist? Well, she didn't want to date someone on speed, and she didn't want to deal with the headache of Dee. I couldn't park my van in front of Leanne's because Dee knew where she lived. When I made the mistake of doing that once, Dee smashed the window and scratched the side of the van.

Leanne and I were at a bowling alley in downtown Portland early one evening. The location made me feel safe, but I was wrong. In came Dee, all attitude and demanding to talk.

Leanne said, "I'm leaving."

"I'll meet you later at your place."

Any time I would try to break up with Dee, she'd go into the same routine, sobbing, "You said that you loved me."

It didn't matter that she kicked me in the head or made a porno film.

"I did love you, but I don't want to be with you anymore," I finally said. Then, I gave Artie the signal to go to the van. He left, and I took off after him. Soon, we were safely cruising down the street.

"I'm sure glad we got away from her," I said.

"Got away from who?" came a voice from the back, and Dee popped out from under the tarps.

Needless to say, I ended up sleeping with Dee that night. It was my only way out. Not long after that, she tried to kill herself by taking a bunch of pills.

My counselor told me I shouldn't talk to her, but I had to. She'd call from different numbers and places, crying and saying it was all my fault. You can imagine what it did to my love life. No girl wants to go out with a guy who has a psycho ex-girlfriend. I didn't know how I'd find a sane girl with an insane girl chasing me.

Leanne tried to help. I was clean for about a week or two so I could show the courts and keep myself out of jail. For about two weeks, I just stayed at Leanne's house and slept. That was the only way that I was going to stay clean. She gave me an ultimatum: either I had to remain clean or she wasn't going to be with me. The first time she tried to leave, I promised never to do it again.

The second time she caught me on speed, I pulled out all the stops—tears and everything. I'd never told anyone before about my mom saying I had a special calling, but I told Leanne in an effort to get her back. I said that I didn't feel that I could live up to the special calling and deal with the pressure. I needed her love and support. It worked, and she stayed with me a second time.

The third time was the last. We went to a wedding on a Friday night, and Leanne and the others were drinking. Here I was a speed addict going to a wedding where I was out of my comfort zone. It had been years since I'd been into alcohol, so I thought it would be okay for me to drink. The next day Artie picked me up to go paint, and I was really hung over. So that meant speed. We got high and went to work as I had so many times in the past. If I hadn't had the alcohol, I would have returned to speed anyway. It was all I knew.

Instead of returning to Leanne's, I went back over to the party house. The next night she walked in when I was getting high with Artie. She looked at me. I looked at her, and she walked off. That was the end of Leanne.

Once she broke up with me, I started spending more time at the party house and ended up with Dee again. It was on and off with her, and although I wanted to be free of her, it was difficult since she was used to partying at the house and knew all of my friends.

I'd been clean for two weeks, and I went back to partying with a vengeance, making up for lost time. When I was with Leanne, I hadn't spent much time at the party house, and now I was ready. DJ Jazz, one of my roommates, had some liquid acid. I'd always heard of people doing acid in their eyes and had wanted to try it. I tipped back my head and held my eye open. When the drop of acid hit my eyeball, it burned. The effect that it had was almost like having a spider web spread open across my eye. I thought he put a lot of drops in there. He said he'd put in only one drop. I had my head in my hands for at least three minutes. Acid usually kicks in slowly and takes thirty to forty minutes—but not that night. The minute I took my hands from my eyes, I was high, and the visual effects were more intense than I'd ever experienced.

There's been an accident
Becky called me at four a.m. and asked me if I could help her with her car. It was broken down on the side of the freeway. It was the middle of the night, and she was afraid of being alone. I told her to relax and said that Artie and I were partying down the road and would be there in ten minutes.

I headed east through the tunnel coming out of down town. She said she was heading west just past the Portland Zoo exit. I saw her car on the opposite side of the freeway and took the zoo exit to turn around. Then I got back on the freeway, came around a slight bend and pulled up behind her vehicle.

"Some tweeker had been working on my car and did something to the carburetor," she said.

"Go sit in the van with Artie," I told her, "and I will try to un-tweek your ride."

I popped the hood and proceeded to the front of the vehicle. With the hood up, I began to examine the engine. I found some duct tape holding together a cable going into the carburetor. It was 4 in the morning, so there was not too much traffic on the road. I had warrants and wanted to get out of there before a friendly officer decided to offer his services.

Out of the corner of my eye, I saw some headlights heading toward me. Next thing I saw was a car passing behind my butt and smashing into the cement guardrail. Wide-eyed, I looked up at Artie and Becky in the van. The looks on their faces were pure shock.

Did that just happen? I asked myself. The car bounced off the cement barrier and began to skid out of control across the freeway. Then it bounced of the inside guardrail. It began to slow down and came to a stop in the middle of the freeway. Around the bend came another car, unaware of the wrecked one in the middle of the freeway. I tried to signal, but it was too late. The second car hit the first, and now there were two wrecked cars in the middle of the freeway.

I got on my cell phone and called 911. "There's an accident west of the tunnel on Highway 26," I said.

"Which tunnel on 26?" the operator asked.

Not remembering that there was another tunnel on Highway 26 on the way to the coast, I said, "The one coming out of Portland."

"What happened?" the operator asked.

"I don't know, but there are a couple of cars in a pileup," I said.

"What is your name?"

I had already given her the information that she needed. There was no way that I was going to give her my name. I hung up the phone.

By the time I got off the phone, there were four cars in the pileup. *Time to go*, I thought. The last thing I needed was the police thinking that it was me on the side of the road who caused the accident. I got into the van and put it into drive. In my side mirror, I saw a truck with a boat coming. I stuck my hand out the window to try and give him some warning. As we pulled around the wreckage, there were four cars, a truck and a boat. Fortunately the people were out of their vehicles, and nobody seemed to be seriously injured.

To me, it looked like maybe the driver had fallen asleep and didn't make the turn. The car came so close to hitting me that I think I could have reached my hand out and touched his bumper.

"Becky," I said. "You're going to need to find someone else to help you get your car," I said.

That wasn't the last time I had to call 911 that week.

Jump for your love

It was about ten p.m., and I was meeting Craig at his girlfriend's apartment downtown to get high. Two things Craig and I had in common: We were not one-woman men, and our girlfriends were crazy. I waited in front of Lori's apartment. It was an older house that had been converted into a three-level apartment with about ten units.

Craig pulled up, and Lori—his girlfriend—jumped out, clearly pissed off. *Here we go again,* I thought. *What did he do this time?* Craig got out, followed by another girl. *Who was this?* I wondered, suddenly interested. *She's cute.*

"What is the problem with Lori?" I asked.

"She's mad that I've been flirting with her friend," he said.

Lori whirled around and started yelling at him. "Damn it, are you coming or not?"

All I wanted to do was get high, so I followed her inside. Craig continued to flirt with the friend and followed slowly. She continued to rant and rave as she walked up the stairs to the second floor.

As I approached the apartment door, I heard screaming like I had never heard before. It sounded like someone was dying. I ran inside to find out what had happened. Lori was nowhere to be found, but the wailing continued. The patio door was slightly opened, and I walked out. I saw a purse sitting in the middle of the patio. The sound was louder out there and I tiptoed to the end, a little afraid off what I was going to see.

I looked over the edge and spotted Lori on the deck below in an unusual position. She continued to scream and cry. Looking down, I could see why. As I looked around, I realized all the other tenants looking out the window staring at me. I had a feeling they thought I might have pushed her. I couldn't figure out how she had gotten down there in the position she was in.

Craig and the friend came out on the patio.

"Go get me a blanket," I shouted. He brought me a blanket, and I jumped down to help her. I put the blanket over her and told her not to move. For the second time that week I was on my cell phone calling 911. When I hung up the phone, I yelled at the girlfriend to get down here and stay with her friend.

"Craig, we need to get out of here before the police come asking questions," I said. The friend came down and we took off. As we were driving away, I could not figure out how Lori had gotten down there in that position. If she had tripped and fallen, she would have been facing the other direction and been farther away from the building.

We called the friend to make sure the paramedics had gotten there and that Lori was all right.

"What happened?" I asked the friend.

"She probably jumped," she said.

"You're kidding, right? Your friend is in the hospital, and you think she jumped?" I didn't buy it. I needed to investigate for myself.

We went back to the apartment, and I began looking for clues. I needed to prove to myself that she didn't jump. The porch was about ten feet by ten feet. It had a tarp on the ground and a metal guardrail that was about one foot high. Not much of a guardrail. I put myself in Lori's shoes and walked out the patio door angry. Her purse was still on the patio, and I noticed that there was a crease in the tarp next to the purse. Things were starting to make more sense to me. She must have run out on the patio and tripped on the crease, dropped the purse and fallen over the edge.

I continued to search for clues and found a broken fingernail on the edge of the patio. I still couldn't figure out how she could have landed in the position she was in. She was facing the building, and the only way that could have happened is if she flipped and twisted. On the deck below, one of the railings was knocked back. She must have hit it with her head, but how?

The friend continued to try and convince me that she jumped. I wasn't buying it. One, why would she jump? Two, if she was trying to kill herself, why would she jump from the second-story patio? It was only about ten feet to the deck below.

The next day my cell phone rang, and it was Lori. I was shocked that she was calling me, but glad because now I could get the truth.

"Are you all right?" I asked.

"The doctors say that I might have broken my back," she said.

In my head, I'm thinking: *You fell from the second floor. You've got to be kidding me, broke your back.*

"I need to tell you something," she continued.

Oh boy, I thought. "What's that, Lori?"

"I think I love you," she said.

"What?"

"I think I love you," she repeated.

"Are you sure you didn't land on your head?" I asked. "Please explain to me why you now think you love me."

"Well, you're the only person who was willing to help me when I was lying there. You jumped down and covered me with a blanket, and you held my hand. You had to beg my friend just to come down and be with me."

This girl is nuts, I thought. "I just have one question," I said. "What happened?"

"Well, I was so mad at Craig when I got into my apartment, so I dropped my purse and walked up to the edge. I jumped off and then realized that I didn't want to kill myself. I turned around and tried to grab the edge."

That must have been how she lost her fingernail, I thought. I couldn't believe it. The friend was right. This girl was nuts.

"I've got another call," I said. "I've got to go."

"Can I call you again?" she begged.

"I guess." *Drugs sure made things interesting*, I thought.

Looking back

Getting out of the situation with Dee, having a place to stay and a new girlfriend who wanted to help me stay clean was an opportunity for me to change. You can't change for other people, though; you have to change for yourself. Although I was starting to think about changing, I wasn't yet able to face the issues that caused my addiction. I thought being clean was just not using drugs that day. I didn't have the skills to stay clean for good. As soon as life got tough, I went right back to using.

CHAPTER TWENTY-SIX
ON THE RUN

The vehicle's stolen. You guys are high. Maybe I should drive.
—Bobby J.

One night I got a call from Leanne. I ended up going over to her place, but in my paranoid state, I was just too nervous to go to bed and couldn't stop looking out the window. I was afraid that Dee would show up at any minute.

It was well known that I liked to have girls at the house. When people would come over for drugs, I'd always say, "Bring all your girlfriends with you." That's how I met Holly. She came over with Brody one night.

She had sandy blonde hair and freckles, and was kind of an earthy, spiritual, marijuana type. *Everything happens for a reason. Earth. Peace. Joy.* If she had done that when we were first talking, it would have been too much for me.

But that night, she and I started talking. I was still feeling bad about Leanne, and I wanted to be straight with Holly. I said that whatever happened with us wasn't love and wasn't going anywhere. I also told her about Dee.

The next day we came home from lunch to get high, and Holly was still in my bed. She said she needed a ride. When we got in the van, she burst into song with the radio. As I said, she was pretty out there.

The next night we were partying around seven o'clock, and Holly called. She said she was just down the street and wanted to drop by. Dee came over that night, and Holly ended up walking home.

Holly wasn't finished though. She'd call me and tell me she had great drugs. I'd drive all the way to her mom's house and go into her room that was full of trinkets and all of the tie-dye stuff. There wouldn't be any drugs, but she'd say the guy was on his way. This happened two or three times before I caught on.

My three addictions were sex, drugs and video poker, and Holly tried to appeal to all three. She couldn't get me with sex anymore. She couldn't get drugs. So she took a shot at video poker. She called me and said she had three thousand dollars. "Would you like to go play video poker?" she asked. Well, of course I did.

I picked her up, and we went to one of the places. We had sex in the van; I couldn't even believe I was doing it. I left her in the van to get dressed and went inside to play. It took me a while, but finally, I lost all of the money.

The next day Holly called me, crying. "I need the money back," she said. "I borrowed it from three or four different people."

In over my head

I was in the hole myself. There was nothing I could do. I owed money to both Brody and Shawn. All I needed to do was just take the money from Shawn and give it to Brody, and take the drugs from Brody and give them to Shawn, but instead I met a girl at a bar and ended up taking her gambling. And no, I didn't win. Furthermore, a guy she introduced me to ripped me off for some drugs and cash. When the money and the girl were gone, I tried to figure out what to do to get myself out of the mess I was in with Brody and Shawn.

Telling the truth was not an option. So I took a few liberties with the truth, making it sound as if the guy who owed me for the drugs and money owed closer to ten thousand dollars than the one thousand or so he owed. That got Brody and Shawn going. They insisted that we go to the guy's place and collect. No one answered our knock on the door. When we looked inside, we could see boxes and suitcases. The guy and his female roommate were moving out. Brody and Shawn decided that we should break in there and take enough to make the guy pay the huge amount I'd led them to believe he owed me.

I climbed up to the second-story balcony, and found the patio door was open. Then, I let Brody and Shawn in. We rummaged through the stuff, his and hers, and took what we thought was real jewelry. Then, we loaded up the van and got out of there. Soon I got a call from my parents' house; the police had been there looking for me.

Brody and I left. When the police got to our party pad, they asked where we were, and Bobby J. said that we'd just left. He also said that I had gotten a phone call and we'd left immediately after. The police returned to my dad's house and arrested him for aiding and abetting. It was a power play to force him to tell them where I was. But my dad didn't have a clue where we were, and they released him. The next day I had my dad take the stuff out of the van and return it to the girl. The police officer who'd arrested him called my cell phone. I was at a softball game when the call came.

"I'm such a gentleman that I'll give you until midnight tonight to turn yourself in," the cop said.

I knew if I got arrested, they'd revoke my probation, and I'd serve six months. With a burglary conviction, it would be worse. There was no way I was going to turn myself in. "If you're such a gentleman, why don't you give me until midnight tomorrow night?" I asked—just to see how serious this was.

The cop had no sense of humor, and I began to worry. I didn't even want to go paint because I was afraid they'd find me. Two days later, Artie was painting where I was supposed to be. About fifteen police officers came, surrounded the house and tackled him to the ground, mistaking him for me. If I needed a sign that they were serious, I had it times fifteen.

Drug running

Brody had been traveling to Canada to get marijuana. I didn't want to leave Portland, but I didn't want to be arrested either. I talked to my friend, Frank, who was Brody's Canadian source. On the run for three years, he was growing marijuana and shipping it back to Portland via Brody. He said I could hide out there and help him.

I drove up with Frank's cousin, Becky. My great escape lasted only three or four days. Frank's life centered on growing and selling marijuana. I was into doing speed. Although Frank and Becky also did speed, partying in Canada was depressing. I didn't know anybody, and I didn't have any money.

Dee had been calling me. Yes, I know we'd broken up, but that didn't stop her, and at that time, it didn't stop me. I had Becky drive me to Bellingham, Washington. Dee met me there and brought me back the rest of the way— about a four-hour drive. Then Dee went back to where she was staying, and I went to my friend Derrick's house.

Halloween was a week away, and Derrick was going to have a big party at his house. I spent the next seven days building a huge turntable stand for the party. It was all I did for a week, just obsessing on building the stand. It filled up the entire front room. I wrapped it in reflective foil, and the turntables sat above black lights within Plexiglas, so that they appeared to be floating. It was the hit of the party, and I was back in my element—for the two days we partied, at least.

A couple of days after Halloween, it happened. It wasn't even noon yet. I was on the couch, putting on my shoes with a weird feeling in my stomach, and I looked out the window. DJ Jazz's stolen 4Runner was parked out in front of the house. An electric company truck moved slowly down the street. When I heard the knock, I thought the electric company people were there demanding that we move the vehicle. Instead they said that they were turning off the power for repairs and asked if we had any computers in the house. Derrick, who'd opened the door, thanked them.

"Actually, we're the Portland Police," one of them said. "Is Mikael Luman here?"

"Just give me one sec." Derrick closed the door, locked it and asked me, "Front or back?"

I already knew who was at the front door. I went out the back. A police officer stood there pointing his gun at me.

"Freeze," he shouted.

I jumped the railing on the deck and hurtled over the six-foot chain-link fence on the back of the property. When I looked back, I saw twelve of them pushing the fence over. As I ran, I glanced periodically to see what was taking place around me. It didn't look good. A police car was stopped on every street.

A guy grabbed me and kind of spun me around, yelling to the cops, "Here he is."

I broke away and ran until I couldn't run any more. Then I hid by the stairs at a church. They were closing in behind me; there was nowhere to go. It was only a matter of time. I just sat there, winded, until they came and got me.

I was charged with the new burglary as well as the probation violations. Once I was finally arrested and in handcuffs, I just fell into a depression and sleep mode. So much fear had built up that once I was in the car, I was almost relieved that I didn't have to be on the run any more.

I went to the hearing for my probation violation, and instead of six months, I got about half that because the jails were overcrowded. I still needed to take care of the burglary charge. I got an attorney and had him ask if there was anything I could do to get the charge dropped since everything I had stolen had been returned. They wanted me to work as an informant. After my three months and twenty-one days, they released me. I received a suspended sentence for the burglary.

Can't get away

During my jail time, I was a trustee and worked in the kitchen as a baker. There were twelve inmates total working in the kitchen. The other baker and I worked from two p.m. to midnight. After the dinner crew left at seven p.m., it was just us and the cook. She liked me and would cook us anything we wanted. Killing time is the biggest challenge in jail. I was always busy baking coffee cakes and cookies for the next day. When I got off at midnight, I'd walk circles around the tank, that is, the dorm area where all the trustees stayed. I'd do that until breakfast and then sleep until my shift. The routine helped the time pass faster.

Two or three days after my arrest, I started receiving letters from Holly—like five or six letters a day. *Peace, love, happiness*—the usual psychobabble. If I'd read one, I'd read them all; they all said the same thing. I got tired of reading them and starting handing them out to the other trustees. Woman-starved as they were, they all wanted to meet her. I told them that they really didn't, that the girl was crazy.

She also called and left messages for me three times at the jail. First, she told the guards that my grandfather was sick, and she needed to talk to me. The second time she told them my cat died and the third, she said my brother had broken his ankle. I begged her to stop. She was only making my life worse.

When I went to court, I was handcuffed to the guy next to me. We inmates, in our little orange costumes, were on one section, and the un-incarcerated people were on the other side. A girl walked in, and all the guys turned to look. Girls were a rarity for us, remember. At first I didn't recognize her. I saw only her attire; there was something wrong about the way she was dressed. *You've got to be kidding me*, I thought. It was Holly, all right. She sailed through the door wearing a long, black dinner dress and matching coat.

I must have moaned because the guys turned to me. "Who's that?" they asked.

"That's Holly," I said.

In one dramatic gesture, she took off her coat, hung it up and then made her way to the front row. The courtroom was full. The bailiff said anyone not there to see the judge had to leave. Holly didn't budge. I was embarrassed that she could see me there in my orange jumpsuit in handcuffs and was glad when the ordeal was over.

Later my attorney said, "I gave your girlfriend a ride home yesterday."

"Dee?" I asked, confused.

"No," he said. "Holly."

Dee had stalked me, but Dee and I had been lovers. Love and peace aside, Holly was like the psycho stalkers you read about. I finally told her to quit calling the jail. If I was lucky, perhaps I'd never hear from her again. Right.

When I got out, I made an agreement with the Washington County drug division to work as an informant. I didn't want to turn in any of my friends, but I wanted to get out of jail on the burglary charge. There was a group of people I planned to focus on, but they weren't really my friends. That's usually how it worked when sharing information with the law.

My best interests weren't necessarily the same as the drug-enforcement peoples' best interests. My probation officer didn't want me hanging around with drug dealers, yet in order to get information, that's what I had to do. When I got out of jail, I was planning on staying clean. I moved into my parents' house but I was clean for only a week. As a result, I met with the drug-enforcement guys only once.

I started using where I'd left off. Artie didn't have a place to stay, so we'd stay at peoples' houses or crash in my painting van. It was February when I got out of jail. My parents had gotten in touch with my probation officer, and they discussed trying to get me into a treatment program. A lot of the programs had waiting lists because there weren't enough beds for the number of people who needed them. I was supposed to check in a couple of different times, but I never did it.

Looking back

As usual, nothing that happened to me was my fault. I was always trying to put the blame on other people, and I was always trying to run away from my problems. If I went to Canada, everything would be fine, I believed. I wouldn't have to worry about going to jail or owning people money. Addicts constantly say that if they can just get away where they don't know anybody, they can get clean. You can't run away from addiction. You have to face it head on.

CHAPTER TWENTY-SEVEN
PARTY LIGHTS

It's all fun and games until you're in handcuffs.
—Mikael Luman, on getting arrested

We used to call the flashing red and blue lights of getting pulled over by a cop party lights, and I saw my share of them. On this night, all I wanted to do was play video poker. Oregon Lottery has rules on the hours of operation of the video poker machines, seven a.m. to two-thirty a.m. It was about two in the morning, and Artie and I walked into Coaches bar wanting to get our poker fix before the machines closed. To our frustration, all the machines were being used.

Jonesing to play, we decided to head down the freeway to the Cheerful Sports Page—the closest bar that we knew was open. I was driving my Ford one-ton cargo van. I had been up for days, and it was difficult enough keeping the van between the lines when I was sober. It was a hard vehicle to drive. We passed a state trooper who was parked on the side of the freeway.

"Artie," I said. "Hide the drugs."

The state trooper weaved through traffic and pulled behind us. The turn signals were out, so I didn't want to change lanes when we approached our exit. I didn't think I was speeding, but it was hard to tell because the speedometer was broken. The cop turned his lights on, and I slowly pulled over. *Not again*, I was thinking. I didn't have warrants at the time, but I didn't have a license, and there were drugs in the van.

"What seems to be the problem, officer?" I asked.

"You were only driving forty-five miles an hour," he said.

"My speedometer is off, and I didn't want to speed."

"You were also weaving back and forth in the lane."

"You try driving this van straight. It's not easy."

"Step out of the vehicle," he said.

Here we go again, I thought.

"Have you been drinking?" he asked.

"I don't drink, officer." I wasn't lying—I hadn't been drinking.

"Can you walk a straight line for me?"

Being up for days made walking a straight line tough, but I gave it my all.

"Hold your hand out to the side and bring one finger to the tip of your nose," he instructed me. "Keep your head facing forward, and follow the light with your eyes."

Speed affects your vision, and I was having trouble with the light.

"You've been drinking," the trooper said.

"I don't drink, officer, I swear. Give me one more chance. Let me try the test again."

"Where are you coming from?" he asked.

"Coaches," I admitted, knowing that it didn't look good coming from a bar and trying to convince the police that I hadn't been drinking.

"Where are you going?"

"The Cheerful Sports Page, but we're just going to play video poker. Like I said, I don't drink."

The trooper asked for my ID and ran my name through his shoulder radio.

"They say you're on probation for drug possession," he said.

"I am," I said.

"Are you high now?" he asked.

"No, I just want to go play video poker."

"Do you know you have a search clause on your probation? If I wanted to, I could search your vehicle."

"I know," I said.

"How about the person with you?" the officer asked. "Who is he?"

"He works for me in my painting business."

"Is he on probation?"

"Yes."

"For drugs?"

"Yes."

"And you don't have any drugs in the van?"

"No. We just play video poker."

"Get back in the vehicle," he ordered.

When I stepped back in the van, I glanced over at Artie, who had a worried look on his face.

"What did he say?" Artie asked.

"He said get back in the vehicle and wait for him. He's probably calling for back up so he can arrest me. Should I run?"

Just then the trooper returned to the van. "Well, I can't sit here and babysit you guys," he said. "You don't have a license, so you shouldn't be driving, but you can do what you want when I leave."

Then he drove off. I was scared to leave. At the same time some Tigard police officers were arresting someone on the other side of the freeway.

"Should we just walk?" I asked Artie. "Can you believe what just happened?"

He shook his head. "No," was all he could say.

If it had been a city police officer, we would have been arrested. This guy was state police, and he probably didn't want to go through the hassle of having to call the city cops. We sat there for what had to be fifteen minutes before I had the courage to start the van and drive away. Even then, my foot was shaking so hard that it was difficult to push it on the accelerator. The officer did me two favors that day. I didn't get arrested, and I finished the night with money in my pocket for a change.

Party's over

Finally, my parents convinced me that I needed to go for an evaluation at the Tigard Recovery Center. I filled out the paperwork that March, but they didn't have a bed. A week later, there was an opening, and my probation officer called my parents. He said if I wasn't at the TRC by noon, he was going to revoke my probation and send me back to jail. I was in a hotel on the other side of town. Dee had been there but had left. My dad knocked on the door and said, "You need to come with me. Your probation officer gave you until noon today to be checked into the rehab center."

"Now really isn't a good time," I said, but there was no arguing with him.

In order to start treatment, patients were supposed to be clean for seventy-two hours. They decided to let me enter anyway. It was tough having to get up early and stay awake during classes. I struggled for the first two or three weeks. The counselors asked if I was serious about my recovery. Up until that time, I hadn't taken it seriously, but after that day, I was convinced that it was in my best interest. If my probation were revoked again, I was going to have to serve the original sentence of twenty-two months—in prison. I just did what I needed to do to get out of rehab. I didn't necessarily do what I needed to in order to stay clean.

In level one, we couldn't leave except to go to AA/NA meetings, and we had to walk together. I was also allowed to go with one of the level-two patients to the gym every day.

At level two, I could leave to go to work, but I still had to be there at night, and I had to go to a certain number of AA/NA meetings. At one of the AA/NA meetings, a girl came in and left. I followed her outside to see why. She had issues with drinking, she said, but felt uncomfortable in the meeting. She lived in an apartment up the street from where the treatment facility was, and the next meeting night, I met her, and we went back to her place. That happened a couple of times while I was there.

Toward the end of level two, I had an opportunity to get out early. There was a big party planned for May 31, and I wanted to be out by then. Although I knew that I didn't want to use speed, I was hoping that I could do ecstasy on the weekends the way I used to. The last month of treatment, I worked hard to complete all of my classes and paperwork. I was released on May 31.

Since I'd been working out, I'd put on a lot of muscle. I was pretty excited to go out because I looked good and felt good. I went with Artie to the rave and did ecstasy and acid. The next morning, we went to after-hours at Derrick's. He and some other guys were smoking coke and heroin. We smoked the rest of the coke in about fifteen minutes and spent the rest of the day running around trying to find more.

I went back to my parents' house that night. The whole next week I was clean, painting a house with Artie. I liked working out at the gym and kind of knew that I didn't want to be taking drugs. Since I wasn't going to use speed, and since I was going to the gym, I reasoned, I might as well hasten the process by using steroids. I couldn't find a connection at the gym, however.

Working and speed were one and the same for me. Artie had been using but kept it away from me. That Sunday, we were going out to a club. Before we left, I begged and begged Artie until he gave me some speed.

My birthday was the following Friday. I was supposed to go paint the next morning, so I used in order to work that day. I didn't want to admit to myself that I was using again. *Okay*, I thought. *I'll party this week, and get clean after my birthday, and everything will be fine.* By the time I got to my birthday, I thought, *Okay, I'll just party through the weekend*. Then, I decided, I'd just party through June and then July 4. By that time, it was too late.

Looking back

You only have so many chances, and you never know which one is your last. That time in jail could have been my last chance. My time in rehab could have been. Although I didn't see it then, today I look at these experiences as miracles that I was still able to have an opportunity to change—that I hadn't done something irreversible. As long as you're alive, it's never too late to change.

CHAPTER TWENTY-EIGHT
MANUFACTURING

Let's just do it one last time, go out with a bang.
I can stop on Monday.
—Mikael Luman, fresh out of rehab

It was July 4. I was still high. My painting time was terminal, I knew. It was only a matter of time before a warrant would be issued. On my last job, my brother's friend loaned Artie and me his truck to go to the paint store. We were really going to get high and go play video poker. The road veered to the right, and I made a blind turn to the left without stopping. Coming around the corner the other way was a Corvette with a D.A.R.E.—Drug Abuse Resistance Education—decal on the side, and I almost sideswiped it. I knew the moment I saw it that it was a police vehicle probably taken in a drug raid. And of course, we had drugs in the car. Because I knew there might be a warrant, I got out of the car so that I could run if I needed to.

"Oh, officer," I said, "that was the dumbest thing I've ever done. I can't believe I did that."

"That was pretty stupid," he said.

"I have to tell you right now, officer, that I don't have a driver's license," I said. "The only reason I'm driving is that we're going to the paint store."

I gave him my name and he said his daughter had gone to school with my brother. "I don't mind if you're driving to go to a paint store," he said, "but don't let me catch you out driving to a girl's house at midnight."

Artie couldn't hear what was going on, and we were in a pickup with a canopy in back, so he couldn't really see. I felt sorry for all of the times I got him in trouble. This day wasn't one of them. We went to play video poker, lost our money and went back to work.

Part of me knew that I would be on the run soon. I was more aggressive about trying to make money, and I convinced my dad to loan me several thousand dollars. I said I'd pay him back the next Monday. I'd hooked up with Adam, who was going to get me a half pound of meth. The plan was to sell it and use the money to get my start manufacturing. The person who was bringing the half pound was supposed to be there at six-thirty. I'd gone with Artie and Brody, but Adam said they didn't want anyone else there. Artie and Brody waited in the car. I was a little nervous, but not too nervous.

Three of them came into the house. They had guns, and the first thing they did was check the other rooms to see if there were people there. I knew right then that something was wrong.

"Do you have the money?" they asked.

"Just let me have the drugs," I said.

"Show us the money."

I gave them the money; they counted it. Then they said they had to go to the car for the drugs. Instead they ran out the back door. I ran out the front door, and Brody and Artie took after them in the car. I headed down a path, cut through some trees and ran out into the middle of the road. They came right at me and I had to get out of the way. They drove on by. Artie and Brody pulled up, I jumped in and we tried to chase them down, but couldn't find them. We went back to Adam's. He still couldn't believe that they ripped us off. I don't know if he had anything to do with it or not. I called people I knew with guns so that we could try to go collect the money they'd stolen.

We went down to where these guys were supposed to be, but they'd just left. I had to tell my dad that I didn't have the money to pay him back. I was even farther in the hole than before. Later I learned that Adam owed them money, and he ripped them off more than they were ripping me off.

I'd started seeing Jenny, a petite blonde who'd always been a weekend party girl but who was just then getting into speed. She had a job at a wireless phone company, and I tried to warn her that if she kept doing speed, she wouldn't be able to keep making it to work. Everybody thinks that they can handle speed and that they're not an addict, but the body can only take it for so long. It was only a couple of weeks before she lost her job, and soon after that she went from a cute girl to not cute at all. She probably lost fifteen pounds and my friends said she looked like Cornelius from *Planet of the Apes.* It was all because of the drugs.

Jenny sent me to the store one night with forty dollars, but instead, I went to play video poker. I had it up to eight hundred dollars, but like an addict, I kept on playing until I lost it all. Three hours later, I had to go back to her place and tell her what happened. When I had cash in my hand, I couldn't resist video poker; my addiction wasn't limited to drugs.

Friendship Versus Addiction

Brody's ex-girlfriend Ren and I were good friends, meaning we always had fun partying together. If I needed drugs, and she had some, she'd share with me. And if she needed drugs, I shared with her. I thought I could trust her.

It was six-thirty in the morning, and Jenny called to see if I had any drugs that I could bring over. I was just dropping off Craig and I told her I'd be there in thirty minutes. Jenny lived in an apartment, and I had to park down from her place. I noticed that Ren's van was parked in front of Jenny's, which was no big deal because we were friends, I thought.

Ren and Jenny were inside. I dropped my backpack on the couch, then went to the bathroom. When I came back out and opened my backpack, there were no drugs. I ran out to my car, thinking they'd fallen out. No drugs. I tried to think of the last person who'd been near my backpack: Craig. I called him and started chewing him out. While we talked, Ren came out of Jenny's apartment. As she was getting into her van, I could see that she was carrying the container that my drugs were in. I hung up the phone and ran toward her van. By the time I got there, she'd gotten it started and put it into drive and accelerated into me. I fell backwards but grabbed onto the windshield wipers. She kept going, driving down the parking lot, swerving back and forth to try to shake me off the van.

When she slowed down for the corner, I took one step on the cement toward the side of the van and threw myself headfirst through her open window, up to my chest. Ren started rolling up the window, my arms still inside. People on their way to work stopped to watch. Somehow, I was able to get my hand on the container and wrest it away from her. Then, I pulled my arms out of the window and got away from the van. She continued to drive off.

It was probably justified in her mind somehow that I owed her or Brody something. Although I saw her after that, she never gave me an explanation. This was just one more lesson for me on how little friendship matters in the drug world.

Looking back
After my time in jail and rehab, I felt that I had a handle on my addiction and could probably use drugs responsibly. I thought I could pick and choose the drugs I wanted to use and when I wanted to use them. With addiction, you never go back to the first time you use; you go back to the last time. When I did drugs for the first time after getting out of rehab, it was as if I had never stopped.

CHAPTER TWENTY-NINE
CHEMISTRY 101

I just want to have the best drugs.
—Mikael Luman, on manufacturing

A lot of the drugs in the scene at that time were coming from Gary—a gun-carrying, hardcore dealer/manufacturer. Gary was one of the reasons I wanted to manufacture for myself. He wasn't the smartest guy in the world, but he was able to repeat the process successfully. Gary was about the money. Although he got high, he didn't really care about the drugs. He just wanted to make as much money as he could.

His meth was kind of a purple-brown color, and it had an iodine taste to it. I tried to get close to him so that he could teach me to manufacture. I'd also developed a few contacts who were taking meth to Canada and trading it for marijuana. Because of the price differences, we could almost triple our money, and I did a couple of deals with Gary. I knew right away that I wasn't going to get much information out of him, though.

If someone would just show me one time how to manufacture, I was certain that I could do it. I'd already picked up a bunch of bits and pieces of information from a lot of sources. I knew that I needed ephedrine, iodine crystals and red phosphorous. Finally, I met a guy named The Kid, who agreed to teach me in return for splitting the profits. He wasn't the typical guy

I would get hooked up with. Just out of jail, he hung out with the bikers. I knew if I stayed around him too long that I would eventually get burned, but I had no intention of doing that.

The first time I manufactured with him was at Jenny's. I had no money, so I used my dad's company checkbook, faked his signature, deposited a fake check and took out a thousand dollars. While we were getting the chemicals we needed, The Kid and I played video poker and spent most of the money. It took about ten thousand dollars to get about two thousand dollars' worth of product.

Rounding up all of the supplies that we needed was a week-long project. Our shopping list included a pressure cooker, funnels, coffee filters, jars, methanol and ether (starter fluid)—both of which we bought at the auto parts store—cotton balls, Red Devil lye and a gas can. We started with the ephedrine. When you take a Sudafed tablet, you aren't getting pure pseudoephedrine; you're getting coloring, bonding agent and all of the ingredients that hold the pill together. That works for you, but it doesn't work for drug manufacturing.

The pills we were buying from the Asian market were pretty clean, but not clean enough. We emptied about twenty-four bottles of pseudoephedrine tablets into the methanol. Since it was a hydrochloride, the ephedrine turned to liquid in the methanol. Once all of the bonding agents and other junk settled to the bottom, we started pouring it through the coffee filters. Once the liquid evaporated, all that would be left was pure ephedrine. We used a microwave so that we wouldn't have to breathe the fumes. The pure ephedrine looked like grainy white powder.

Hydriatic acid was our reducing agent. It's close to impossible to get, so we used the iodine crystals and red phosphorous to create it. This is where manufacturing can get dangerous. A percentage of water, a percentage of iodine crystals and a percentage of red phosphorous combined in a gas can create an explosive hydrogen-iodine gas contained in the water. I could almost hear the energy inside the gas can as it swelled and then went back down. Most of the smoke was trapped in the can, but when we uncapped it, we nearly choked on the pungent fumes.

We used a jar with a screw-on lid and poured ephedrine, red phosphorous and the contents of the gas can inside it. We then put this jar of purple liquid inside the pressure cooker, which we'd filled with water. The Kid said that we needed to run the cooker at thirty pounds of pressure for six hours. Once we got the pressure up to about twenty-five, the seal on the cooker started to weaken, and steam started shooting out. Yet we couldn't stop the process. We tried to tape it up, but with thirty pounds of pressure, it was difficult. The six hours became two hours in a hurry.

We ended up with a red layer at the bottom and a purplish/gold liquid above. Then we took that liquid and put it into a plastic milk jug along with the ether. To that, we added the lye mixed with water. The methamphetamine rose into the ether. Then we took the ether off the top and put into a different container with distilled water. To that, we added hydrochloric acid and shook it. Then we poured off the water through a filter into a jar and dried this final mixture in a glass baking dish on the stove. As the water evaporated, it thickened and became crystalized. Instant meth—well, not all that instant. I needed to sample it first.

Once we dried off the first amount, The Kid took only that and asked if he could leave in my van. I was okay with it; all I was interested in was the meth. I knew there was at least half an ounce left, if not more. Repeating what I had seen him do, I went through the steps. I was upset that the result wasn't clear, but then The Kid's wasn't clear either. As long as I could smoke it and get high, I was happy with that result and knew that I could refine the process with practice.

After I was finished manufacturing this first batch, I was eager to sell what I had. I didn't have my van—The Kid had borrowed it and hadn't brought it back—and I didn't dare ask my dad for more money. So, I borrowed a car and went to all of the places where The Kid might be and finally tracked down the van at one of the houses he'd taken me before. He wasn't there, so I had to get a spare key from my dad. Throughout the next six months, I continued to hear stories of The Kid borrowing somebody's car and not returning it. I never saw him again.

Before I left Jenny's house that first time, I cleaned it up and threw everything away and ended the relationship with her. Some people move slowly into addiction, as I did; others rush into it with open arms. Jenny was one of the scary ones. As sick as I was, I knew that she would only bring me down.

Usually I hated trying to leave a girl, as was witnessed by my on-off relationship with Dee. Breaking up with Jenny was pretty easy. The drugs already mattered more to her than I did, and she soon found a new interest in creepy Gary. He'd always liked bringing girls out to the barn where he was manufacturing and having them do the work for him. Even before we broke up, Jenny was out there with him. After she and I stopped seeing each other, she hooked up with him.

I had no money, and I was not painting for my dad. All I wanted to do was manufacture. That meant I needed Brody's help. Yet, Brody and I were not on the best of terms. We met, but he wanted to bring in Trey to help us. I was upset that Brody didn't trust me enough. I didn't want to bring in one other person. Besides, I didn't really trust Trey.

Artie got angry and said, "If they're willing to help you, dude, team up with them and let them. Quit acting like the man. You aren't the man any more."

My pride wouldn't let me consider what he was saying. I was hanging out with the guy who hooked me up with The Kid. My bridges were pretty much burned as far as money was concerned. Then I heard that Gary had thirty pounds of ephedrine in the barn where he manufactured. If I had that, I knew I could trade it for the other products that I needed.

Career criminal

I called Nate, whom I'd known for several years. Nate, who hadn't worked since I'd met him, lived with his girlfriend; she didn't have a clue about his second life. Without her knowing, he dated one of Dee's friends for years, and was the guy in the strip club parking lot who Faith—Joe's girl—was seen fooling around with. In the past, Nate and I had gone and stole various things together. Holly's ex-boyfriend was another of our targets.

Holly said that he left his door unlocked. Armed with tasers, Nate and I broke into his house and stole some electronics, among other items. We left, and I returned for more stuff. I came in the back patio door and didn't realize that Holly's ex had come home and was upstairs in the shower. I heard the shower turn off and sneaked out the back.

On this night I told Nate about Gary's ephedrine. We scoped out the place, well aware that Gary was armed and dangerous. Gary had a place on the east side and the west side of Portland. The latter was where he did the manufacturing. He always carried about thirty grand in cash hidden in his car. Stealing it was too risky, so we decided to steal the ephedrine from the barn.

Nate came back that night with all of the gear—camo pants, camo jackets, hoods. It was clear that he'd done this kind of stuff before. We headed for his house, drove by it and could see Gary's car in the front. The barn was thirty yards away from the house. We parked down the street and went through a field to the back side of the property. There were no doors on that side of the barn, but we could see through the boards that nobody was in there. As we neared the front, we saw a pickup truck in front with trash in the back. There was a lock on the barn, but that didn't stop me. I knew how to pick locks.

I was pretty scared. All I had was a taser, and I knew Gary had a gun. The only way out was through the front, so I had Nate stay there. I looked everywhere but couldn't find the ephedrine, but I did discover five or six guns. I figured they were better than nothing, so I stole them.

Although I sold the guns, the money didn't go to manufacturing. I lost it all on video poker. So basically, I risked my life for nothing. Again, I was broke and without a plan.

I started dating Vanessa, an Asian woman I met through some dancer friends of mine. There were two dancer groups: Dee's group from the strip bars, and another group whose members danced at the lingerie shops. Two or three girls worked at a time in a house. A man would come in by himself and pay a hundred bucks for a girl to meet him in the room. The more the man paid, the more clothes the girl took off, and the more "exotic" the dance got.

This second group called me "Sparkles" because they said the first time I met them, when I was high on ecstasy, I looked as if I were sparkling. Mack's girlfriend was part of this group, and they weren't friends with Dee's group. Anywhere else I went, Dee would find me. This group was safe for me; they protected me from her.

I had no place to stay and no money for drugs. I figured if I got hooked up with a stripper girl, I'd have both. Soon I was staying at Vanessa's, but I still needed a way to come up with some money. A few years before, I was knocked down by a falling board at Home Depot. Joe, the scammer, insisted that I pursue it and put me in touch with his attorney. I needed the receipt from Trey's aunt to prove that I was in the store. She said she'd give it to me only if I'd give her half. I said no way. Now, the attorney called out of the blue and said Home Depot was finally ready to settle for only a couple of grand since I couldn't get the receipt.

Bobby J. had a place in Beaverton. He'd naturally progressed into dealing because of a contact he had. Although he'd never wanted to be a dealer, he had such a good product that he was dealing before he knew it. He and Brianna had broken up, another stripper situation gone sour. He asked me if Vanessa had a friend he could date. Vanessa was cute, but her friend Marianne was a knockout. I asked Vanessa if she and Marianne wanted to party at Bobby J.'s, and in the back of my mind, I was wondering how I could get rid of Vanessa and be with Marianne.

When we got to Bobby J.'s, I told him I was interested in Marianne and suggested he take Vanessa. The dancers were all into muscle relaxants and they gave us some. Bobby J. and I passed out, and the girls left, so nothing happened. Later, Bobby J. and Marianne got together. But he still had Brianna the way I still had Dee, and Marianne got tired of that really fast.

Bobby J. didn't have a problem with video poker. When he got high, he liked to go to Value Village, a second-hand store. He could spend hours and come out with a couple of shirts and a pot or pan. He liked going in and finding a treasure. I was confident that if I asked him to hang on to my settlement money, he would. I didn't trust myself.

He helped me get the ephedrine, the iodine and red phosphorous. He didn't want me to run the reaction at his house but said that it was okay if I pulled the pills there. The only place I had to do it was Vanessa's. I pulled the pills at Bobby J.'s. Now all I had to do was add the chemicals and put them in the pressure cooker. Artie and Vanessa were there. This was only my second time and I didn't have a lot of experience.

About three hours into it, the pressure-release valve popped off. Steam and water shot out of the top, and a piercing noise filled the apartment. Artie was like a deer in headlights. I ran in there, yanked the pressure cooker off the stove and stuck it in the oven. Then I tried to clean up as much as possible. Artie just stared out the window, convinced someone was coming. At that point, I decided to leave the whole mess in the oven and just go out for a while.

Brody found out that I was staying at Vanessa's. He went through one of the back windows and stole the reaction. From what I heard, he messed it up and ended up not getting any product out of it.

Looking back

Although I'd had lows as well as highs in my addiction, this was my lowest point. I was getting farther out of control than I'd ever been before. The new people I hung out with and the things I started doing were rock bottom. I was pretty much willing to do whatever it took to survive—lie, steal, risk my own life.

CHAPTER THIRTY
THE MAN WHO CAN

If I can't be the best at being good,
I can still be the best at making meth.
—Mikael Luman, justifying manufacturing

I called Trey and told him what happened. My only option was to work with Trey, but without Brody. Trey was fairly knowledgeable, and he knew people who were more so. Remember, Trey and Dee were best friends, so that meant Dee was back in my life. She couldn't wait to put Vanessa down. That's what she did with every woman I dated. In her mind, every woman I was involved with was ugly and a slut. Vanessa and I were finished anyway, but even though Dee and I were kind of back together, the one I wanted was Marianne.

Trey owed me thousands of dollars that I'd never collected on. He was the kind of guy who'd ask me to go out and pick up on girls and then tell Dee what we did. He was also unreliable, dishonest and incapable of loyalty, and his memory must have been as short as he was because he could stab you in the back and then turn you around to ask if you were all right.

Trey liked working out of hotels; he didn't want to manufacture at home. Instead of a pressure cooker, he used the old-fashioned method of a flask and a condenser. Instead of six hours, this method required twenty-four to thirty-six hours. We would get the process started and leave the hotel room. For the sake of security, we'd stick a piece of paper in the top of the door. That way, if the paper was gone when we returned, we'd know not to go inside the room.

When I first started working with him, Trey had me doing only the dirty work like cleaning or setting up. His dope was like he was—kind of sludgy. And no matter what he did, it always came out the same. After about a month we hooked up with a tow truck driver who had a repair shop outside of town. It was a better situation than the hotel room, but there were no windows in the front, and it was dark and cold. Not an ideal situation but less risk, we reasoned. Trey would drop me off there and say he'd be back in four hours. Twelve hours was more like it. He left me there all New Year's Eve. The place had no heat, and there was nothing for me to do but call him on the cell phone.

Right before New Year's, Marianne called me from her parents' house because Bobby J. and Brianna were back together. There'd been a vibe between us the night we met. She mentioned that she was going to a rave in Seattle the weekend following New Year's Day. New Year's Eve was on a Thursday, and the rave was on a Saturday, January 2. Trey had left me at the shop until six in the morning. I was cold and pissed, but I had no choice but to help him. I had nothing but the clothes I was wearing and a backpack.

He had been partying for several days and fell asleep at the beginning of the process. I'd talked him into using a pressure cooker instead of the flask and condenser that he swore by. I ran the reaction, and when I couldn't wake him, I continued. When he finally woke up, I was drying and crystallizing the batch. My dope consisted of chunky, big crystals, much better looking than Trey's. Surprisingly, he did not get angry. Instead, he called me "the man who can." This was the first time I'd actually manufactured by myself. I'd done it with Trey, with The Kid, but never solo. I felt I knew what I was doing, and now I had proof. We were both pretty excited.

I told him I wanted to go to Seattle, and he bought me a plane ticket. It was the way he kept control of me, doing something nice after mistreating me. It was also a nice way to separate me from the drugs I'd just made. I stashed some drugs in my sock and flew to Seattle. Marianne and several guy friends of hers picked me up at the airport. We got high, and I could tell that one of the guys was upset that I was there.

I finally got her away from the guys and spent the money Trey gave me buying ecstasy. The next day at the airport, I realized I didn't have enough to buy a ticket. It was embarrassing, but I had to ask Marianne to buy my plane ticket. We flew back together, then hung out at her house for a while and then fell asleep. Trey had been calling me, but I'd slept through it. My job was to pull the ephedrine. That day, Trey got tired of waiting and did it himself. He'd bought some pills with a different bonding agent.

When I got there and looked at the pooled ephedrine, I said, "Trey, there's junk in there. We can't run it."

He was convinced that the ephedrine was fine. He started running the reaction, and we didn't get anything. Twenty-five hundred dollars of investment would have been fifteen to twenty thousand in profit, and he blew it. He was involved in a custody battle for his daughter and needed money to pay his attorney. This money was supposed to go for that. He got angry and left me at the shop as punishment. I called Marianne to come pick me up. That was the first night that we were intimate.

The tow truck driver had gone to jail, and we were supposed to pay the rent for the shop. I didn't have the money to pay him, and Trey didn't either after he ruined the batch. I was crashed out at Marianne's. At that point, I was so fed up that I didn't care if I worked with Trey again.

The owner of the shop saw the stuff that was in there. He told Trey if we didn't get it out in twelve hours, he was calling the police. Trey didn't even go himself. He sent Pinkie to come pick me up, and at about two in the morning, we went to the shop. We were afraid it was a trap, so we scoped out the place first. No one was there, so we got our things out in a hurry.

Here we go again

Trey told Dee about Marianne, and that was all it took for Dee to fly into one of her rages. Dee contacted Marianne immediately, and Marianne came over to Trey's house angry and ready to break up with me. I convinced her that it was over between Dee and me and that I loved her.

Trey and I both needed money, so we got a hotel room in Vancouver, Washington. I was in the upstairs loft and had just finished getting the pills pulled, when Dee came knocking on the door. Her best friend, Jane, was with her. Jane knew how crazy Dee was and always took my side. I couldn't believe that she'd bring Dee to the hotel.

She managed to act normal for about two seconds. The minute the door was closed, she started screaming, cussing and knocking things down.

"I don't want to be with you anymore," I told her.

"But you said you loved me."

It was the same conversation we had any time she went into a rage.

One, I had warrants. Two, I was manufacturing. There was no way I could let her do this.

"Get her out of here," I told Jane. But that didn't work.

Dee kept swinging and trying to hit me. She completely snapped. I was certain that someone would call the police any minute. I finally grabbed her and sat her into a chair. That didn't help much, but it did get her still. I then got Jane to come over and calm her down. I went back upstairs and started cleaning up in case the cops broke in at any minute. After ten or fifteen very long minutes, Jane finally got Dee calmed down, and they left.

The only way Dee could have known where to find me was through Trey. I called him on his cell and started yelling at him. I was starting to see him for what he was. He liked to create drama, even when that drama threatened my business and my life. He had to have known what Dee would do.

"I didn't tell Dee," he said. "I just told Jane."

He had to know Jane would tell Dee. I'd had just about enough of him.

Marianne came to stay that night at the hotel. I was in bed asleep, and she was lying with me when it happened. The next thing I knew, there was a gun in my face. It took me a minute to realize what was happening.

"So you owe this girl some money?" the guy asked.

"What?" I said.

"You owe this girl some money," he repeated, louder this time.

Finally, I looked past him and saw Dee standing by the stairs to the loft. The look on her face was one of the most vindictive, evil expressions I'd ever seen.

The guy saw the look, and it began to dawn on him that Dee had lied to get him there.

"Dude," I said. "I don't know what she told you, but I don't owe her anything."

"I'm not leaving here until I get paid," he said.

The guy didn't care. He had a gun. He was pointing it at me, and he wasn't leaving without any money. At that point, Trey came in, and as soon as he saw that the guy had a gun, he pulled his gun.

Dee's vindictive look was replaced by one of fear.

"Put your gun away!" the guy shouted.

"You put yours away, or I'll shoot," Trey told him.

Their bluffing was like a poker game, only loud and heated.

Marianne went downstairs to talk to Dee. I didn't want to imagine what lies Dee would be telling her. I was losing a girlfriend. I had a gun to my head. I didn't know how my life could get any worse. But it would.

Trey and the gunman finally stopped shouting and worked out some kind of payment arrangement. The gunman took off. Dee left mad. I was stuck with the job of trying to convince Marianne that I'd been faithful to her. I couldn't believe this was happening, and it was all because of Trey. Because he couldn't keep his mouth shut, and because he had to stroke his short-man ego any time he could.

I should've cut him loose. I should have forgotten I ever knew him. But I was dependent on him and stuck in the situation. I was addicted to drugs and addicted to gambling, and I needed money for both. Besides, even though he was a jerk, I felt sorry for him because of his custody battle for his daughter. As scary as the idea of Trey as a parent might have seemed, the alternative was worse, and I knew that he loved his daughter. There were plenty of times with him that were good, and I tended to remember those more than the bad.

Throughout this period, I'd gone to talk to Pinkie if I had trouble with Trey. Even though he was Trey's father, Pinkie was always on my side. He knew that his son didn't care about anybody but himself. Still, Pinkie couldn't say much because Trey was giving him a place to live. After Trey lost the bar, Pinkie, who had been living in his van outside the bar, had moved in with him.

The house that Trey lived in had a little attic off the upstairs part, and Pinkie had turned it into a room. I visited there a lot to talk to Pinkie. I was interested in how he got from where he started to a drug addict living in an attic. Also, I liked the guy. He probably used Vietnam to do whatever he wanted to with the drugs. But he was a decent person and good with Trey's daughter. Unless you knew him, though, he wasn't the kind of guy you wanted to be friends with.

Looking back

I thought that once I learned how to manufacture, life would be okay again. I'd have money, drugs, friends, and I wouldn't have to go from house to house. I'd be the man again. Manufacturing didn't change my life drastically, however. I still hadn't dealt with the other issues in my life, and I continued to slip farther and farther away from everything I valued.

CHAPTER THIRTY-ONE
KIDNAPPED

You remind me of myself when I was your age.
—Biggs, to Mikael Luman

One night I left Trey's to go play video poker. When I returned, Biggs was at Trey's house. When I was getting drugs from Joseph and Hank, Biggs was one of Hank's friends. A former member of the Gypsy Joker biker gang, Biggs was about six-five, three hundred fifty pounds, a little overweight but still in good shape—and massive. He had dark hair, longer in the back, and a Fu Manchu moustache.

Trey had told him that it was my fault that Trey needed money. I came in the door, and Biggs grabbed me and threw me into the garage. I quickly realized that he wasn't joking. He picked up a hammer and started shoving me around, pushing me into the garage door. I was more scared than I'd been with the guy holding the gun on me in the hotel room. This situation was a lot more intense, and it lasted a lot longer.

He accused me of f-ing up Trey's business, calling me irresponsible.

"How I am I messing up Trey's business?" I asked. "I'm the one who's helping out."

Once he calmed down, Trey decided that I should go back to Washington with Biggs to manufacture. I think that was Trey's intention the whole time. He said he'd be coming up to work with us as well. Biggs lived on some property that was thirty minutes out of town. It was an ideal place to manufacture. Since Trey and I were running out of options and places to go, it was a natural next move.

I went up there with Biggs and most of the supplies. Trey was going to bring up the rest of the stuff separately. He had a damaged car parked out in front of his house. He was supposed to tow it and bring the rest of the supplies with him that night. My job was to pull the pills and get the mixture ready to run the reaction. Trey came that night, dropped off the car and the supplies, and said he'd be back in six hours to start running the reaction. Twenty-four hours later, he still hadn't come back.

"Just let me run the reaction," I said to Biggs.

"No," he said. "Trey said you don't know what you're doing. We're waiting for him."

Trey ended up getting pulled over and taken to jail. I convinced Biggs to let me run the reaction, and finally, he agreed.

"You really do know what you're doing," he said when I finished.

He knew then that Trey had been lying. He also kind of apologized for the event in the garage. It was clear that Trey had been playing him. He could now see how easy it would be for him to slide into Trey's place.

We finished that batch of drugs. Biggs packaged them, left me enough to get high with and said that he was going to sell it. He was gone for seven days, and I was stuck without money and with very little food. Marianne came up to see me and brought me some food. I thought Biggs would be coming back sooner and we were going to split the money. When he finally returned, he had a story about what had taken him so long. He should have come back with a lot more money than he did, and he didn't give me any of it.

"We have to use this to manufacture more," he told me. Without missing a beat, he had stepped into Trey's role.

We rounded up the stuff that we needed to manufacture some more. This time it was going to be split fifty-fifty, we agreed. I manufactured more, and he ended up doing the same thing again—taking the product and leaving for seven days. When he came back, he had another story about why he couldn't split the money.

Before this, he didn't have much. He was driving a junker car and was paying only about four hundred dollars a month for rent. This was a good opportunity for him to make money. Finally, I knew that I was getting really good at manufacturing and that I could find somebody else to front me the money. At that time, Bobby J. was also dealing, and I figured that he would probably do it.

Bigg problems

Biggs always slept on the couch by the front door, and I swear he always slept with one eye open. Once when he was asleep, I snuck out of one of the back windows. Then, I went to the restaurant down the street and called Artie to come get me. He did, and then he took me to Marianne's house. I was there several days.

One afternoon Artie and I decided to walk down to the store. When we came back, Marianne's front door was cracked open. We went inside to find Biggs. He had another guy with him and had grabbed Marianne by the arm. I could tell she was freaked out.

"Either you come with me," Biggs said, "or we'll take her."

"I'll go," I said.

I left with him and the other guy in a pickup. I noticed a bag in the truck. It was full of different tools, Biggs said, and he was going to cut my fingers off if I tried to leave. He'd stolen four hundred dollars from Marianne's purse, so she got in her car with Artie and was following us on the freeway. A couple of times she was right behind us and Biggs slammed on the brakes, forcing her to do the same.

When we got to Washington, Biggs told the guy with me to take me inside. The guy grabbed me. Marianne ran up to Biggs and sprayed him with mace. He tore inside, furious. She finally left without her money. My dad called me that night and asked if I was alright. I said I was. Telling the truth would have been too dangerous.

Biggs let me know that I wasn't going anywhere. I was there, I was going to manufacture, and I really didn't have a choice in the matter. It's weird how drug addicts see things as different from what they really are.

Biggs had no claim to the money from those drugs, and he really had no way to keep me in Washington. Yet I was afraid to leave. He threatened me, and in conversation, he would kind of throw out my parents' address, along with what he was willing to do to them. He was like Trey in the fact that he could be my best friend one moment, and in the next, he would be hitting me in the ribs with a baseball bat. An hour later, he'd be wrapping my ribs with an Ace bandage asking if I was all right. I was more afraid of what would happen if I left than if I stayed.

He manipulated Marianne to a point that she was almost on his side and felt that I should remain there. In spite of his stealing from her, she began coming up to visit me. There were times that he let me go back down to stay at her house. But even then, I knew that I'd better be back when I said I would. If I wasn't, he would just come and get me.

Early that summer, Marianne got pregnant. For some reason, I was okay with it. In the past, abortion was an option I had used, and although I had mixed feelings, I felt it was for the best at the time. Now, I knew that sooner or later, I was going to have to serve twenty-two months, but I wanted to be around—clean and not using—when the baby was born. Marianne and I never discussed abortion; we knew we were going to have this child.

When Biggs found out that Marianne was pregnant, he said things like, "You'd better not keep that baby away from me, or I'll have to kill you." He acted as if we'd be one big, happy, dysfunctional family, but I knew better. I had no intention of letting him ever get near my child. If I didn't have the motivation to escape from him before, I did now.

Looking back

Most people take having a baby as a life-changing event, but I did just the opposite. I felt that I was past the point of no return, and I used Marianne's pregnancy as an excuse to get more out of control. We all kind of judge our addictions along the way. At that point, I'd broken all of my rules. I was stealing from family and friends as well as people I didn't know—anybody. I was a full-fledged addict with no desire to change.

CHAPTER THIRTY-TWO
LIFE ON THE RUN

The man is brilliant. And for a criminal lifestyle, that is not good.
—Bobby J.

I knew I had to get out of the situation with Biggs, but I needed a plan. Around this time, I convinced him to let Artie come and stay. He needed a place, and I felt that he would help diffuse the violent situation with Biggs. I was tired of getting hit with baseball bats.

There were times that Biggs would leave for days at a time. At one of those times, one of the women he sold to—the woman who'd given him his Ford Expedition—had come by. Her name was Pat, and she was the female equivalent of Trey or Biggs. She ranted that day that Biggs had taken a girl who was supposed to be selling drugs for her with him when he left. The girl was having a good time with him and not returning Pat's phone calls.

When people had come over before, I never said much, and Biggs took the credit for manufacturing. That day, feeling I had a receptive audience, I told Pat the truth about what was going on—that I was the one who was manufacturing, and that he was more or less keeping me captive. She said that she'd try to help me out in return for drugs.

When Biggs came back, he had a feeling that something was going on. We left in the Expedition, and when we returned, he said, "Don't go inside."

"What's wrong?" I asked.

"Nothing. Just sit here."

After twenty minutes, I said, "If we're going to sit here all night, can I at least get high?"

He said okay, and we sat there smoking crystal.

Pretty soon a car drove by. "Did you see that car?" he demanded.

I thought he was just tweaking, being paranoid, but then a car came back the other direction.

"If you're so worried about the car," I said, "why don't you just follow it?"

We were about two hundred yards behind the car on the freeway. "Biggs," I said. "Are you just going to follow them, or are you going to pull up next to them and see if it's who you think it is?"

We pulled up beside the car on the driver's side. I looked over, and to me, the people inside just looked like somebody's grandparents.

"Look," I said. "They're just old people. You're tripping out. We followed them for five miles, and it's just Grandma and Grandpa."

They slowed down, and we pulled ahead, because we were going to take the next exit and go home. But then, the car picked up speed, and in a second, it was right next to us on Biggs' side.

"Check this out," he said.

I looked across him, but all I could see was an old man and woman. The next moment, every window in the Expedition was shot out. I had my head down, and Biggs sped up. By the time I looked, the car was way behind us.

We made it back to Biggs' house about midnight, unable to figure out who would shoot at us.

Artie was there and when he got me alone, he said, "Pat called, trying to reach you. She said to stay away from Biggs tonight."

At the time, I didn't connect the warning to what had happened on the freeway. When I went out and looked at the Expedition the next day, I saw that the metal strip between the driver's door and the back passenger's door had two bullets stuck in it. That's how close Biggs had come to being shot. I could also see that a bullet had gone through the driver's window and exited through the passenger window not far from where my head had been. We finally chalked it up to a random act of violence, and I knew that I could no longer put off getting out of there.

Escaping Ridgefield

Marianne had left to go to Hawaii with her parents, and they were flying back in. I asked Biggs if I could take the Expedition to go pick her up at the airport.

I wasn't excited about driving the bullet-damaged Expedition, but it was my only option. I picked up Marianne, and she asked if I could give her parents a ride to their car.

"That's not such a good idea," I said.

She got in the truck, and I explained to her what had happened.

I stayed with her that night in her new apartment and told her a little about my exit plan.

"Stay away from Biggs," I said. "Don't call there or try to contact me."

I didn't want her to be in jeopardy. She had moved, so I wasn't all that worried that he'd track her down the way he had before. I was concerned, however, that he'd talk her into coming to Washington or revealing her whereabouts. He was a master manipulator and very good at changing the facts around to get what he wanted.

The next time Biggs left, I started cleaning up the house. Anything that had to do with manufacturing was wiped down and put away. Five or six days after the shooting, two girls who manufactured for Pat came up to Ridgefield, Washington. They told me that she was in jail for possession and distribution. Their names were Kelly and Shannon; I met them at a restaurant down the street. Kelly, a slender blonde, did most of the talking. I told them I needed to get away from Biggs.

"The Gypsy Jokers aren't about that kind of stuff," she said. "If he was doing that to you, he was doing it on his own. I'll put you in touch with the president of the Jokers, and he'll help you."

We went back to the house and picked up Artie. I didn't want to take everything of mine that was there because I didn't want Biggs to think that I had ripped him off. I took about twenty pounds of iodine so that I'd have something to bargain with, and we left.

When we got to Beaverton, Kelly introduced me to Backlash—Shannon's boyfriend and the father of Kelly's child. The guy was in his fifties, but he obviously got around. He had short hair, talked with a raspy voice and had earned his name because he punched first and so hard. An avid smoker of cigarettes and crystal, he had a persistent cough that made him appear a little sickly.

I met him at Kelly's house in Beaverton. We sat down together, and I told him what had happened with Biggs. He was outraged about what Biggs had done; it wasn't true to the Jokers' code, he told me.

He had a huge gold ring on his finger with a joker on it. "You know what this ring means?" he asked. "It means that I was president of the Gypsy Jokers. We have our own rules, and don't believe in kidnapping and taking advantage of innocent people."

Biggs probably wasn't a member of the Jokers, he said, and if he was, he still didn't have permission from the membership to kidnap me.

Upset as he was that Biggs was giving the Jokers a bad name, Backlash still wasn't going to help me just to be nice; I had to give him something in return. He asked what I could do for him, and I said that I was one of the most knowledgeable manufacturers around. I told him that I could probably double the return he got on his ephedrine, and I could help him make a better product.

In return, he was going to go up to Ridgefield with me to get my things and to set Biggs straight. Right after this, I was back at Kelly's with Backlash, the girls and another biker named Buzz.

"I can't believe that you shot with this boy in the car," Backlash said to Buzz. "It really pisses me off that you'd do anything that stupid. Who gave you the authority anyway?"

I listened, shocked, realizing that I was face to face with the guy who'd shot at us. And I thought it had been two old people!

"I wasn't after him," Buzz said. "Pat and her old man were in the front seat wearing wigs and glasses. I was in the back with the gun."

"Pat doesn't have the authority to order a hit," Backlash said. "You could have killed this boy. You're always too willing to pull the trigger without thinking."

As they argued, I learned that Buzz had a history of shooting people. The only reason Biggs was able to get so far ahead at the end was because Buzz needed to get rid of the gear, so they slowed down. What I'd witnessed on the freeway at way too close a range was an attempted hit. I was blown away. I'd asked Pat for her help, not to kill Biggs.

Artie, Backlash and I got in the car and headed for Washington. When we got to Biggs', we went up the driveway. Before we got to the door, Biggs cracked open the blinds so that he could see us.

Backlash said, "I'm here to get the boy's things."

"None of his stuff is here," Biggs said. "He tried to get me busted by leaving his crap all over the place."

"I really don't care about all that." Backlash flashed his ring. "What do you mean saying you're a Gypsy Joker?"

Biggs instantly changed. He started talking about some bikers who had died in the past and tried to pretend that he knew them. "Why don't you come back tomorrow, and we can talk."

"I'll be back," Backlash said. "You'd better have the boy's stuff ready."

We turned around and got in the car. I tried to get in touch with Marianne, but she wasn't answering her phone. On a hunch, I asked Backlash to go by Biggs' again. Marianne's car was parked there. Finally, I reached her on the phone, and I realized that Biggs had brainwashed her and made it sound as if I were the one in the wrong. I finally convinced her that she needed to get out of there. From the time I told her that I was leaving Biggs', I hadn't called her. I thought that if she didn't realize where I was, Biggs couldn't harm her. She'd gone to his place because she thought I'd be there. He'd tricked her again.

As she promised, Marianne left that night, and we went back the next day. Biggs had moved out, taking everything with him.

Looking back

Being kidnapped by Biggs was a frightening experience, but I'd been kidnapped by addiction for years. I could have gone to my parents or to rehab. I could have turned myself in or called the police. But my addiction ruled, and I still wanted to manufacture. Thus, I traded a bad situation for one that was almost as bad. I knew that sooner or later the consequences of my actions would come crashing down on me, but I wanted to prolong the inevitable as long as I could.

CHAPTER THIRTY-THREE
LLOYD AND UNCLE RICK

I'm fine using ecstasy. I just need to stay away from speed.
—Mikael Luman, after rehab

I was finally out of the situation with Biggs, but I'd been catapulted into a relationship with Backlash, Kelly and Pat, who was still in jail. Into the mix came this guy named Lloyd. An exterminator by trade, he was in his early fifties, with gray hair and a pear-shaped body—big around the middle and skinny on top. Apparently the Expedition that Pat had given Biggs was really rented from Enterprise by Lloyd. He was the one whose name was on Kelly's and Pat's rented homes.

People in the drug business will take advantage of anyone, and Lloyd was one of those people who made good prey—new to the drug world and willing to buy friendships and get drugs. At one time, he was paying for three rental cars for three different people. The vehicle that Pat was driving when we got shot at was rented by him as well. Not only did one of his rented vehicles get shot at by the other, but Biggs had absconded in the Expedition.

Artie and I moved into Pat's house with Backlash and a couple of other people. Pat wasn't happy that we were in the house, but we didn't really care since she was in jail, and Lloyd, who was paying the rent, said we could.

I liked hanging out with Lloyd. He'd gotten into drugs at an older age and had good stories. Another thing that intrigued me was that like me, he was Christian when he was younger. He confessed to me that he had been the other person in the vehicle with Pat, her biker friend and Buzz when we were shot at. He hadn't known me at the time and felt terrible about how close I'd come to being killed.

Lloyd told the car rental company that the Expedition was stolen. For the next few days, the security people from the rental company followed us and took pictures—presumably to make sure that Lloyd hadn't lied about the car being taken. They also insisted that Lloyd turn in his other car rentals.

Biggs was arrested in a Washington hotel, and the Expedition was returned to the car company. They questioned Lloyd about the bullet holes, and he said he had no idea how they got there.

When I got to Pat's house with Backlash, I needed to fulfill my promise regarding helping him improve his manufacturing. I'd never retrieved my equipment from Biggs'. Backlash and his friends would use whatever they could—a milk jar or a two-liter jug. I was used to using the proper equipment, but I had no choice but to suck it up and do the best I could with what they had.

When I went to run the reaction, before I put the lid on the pressure cooker, one of the four glass beer bottles exploded, and a glass shard cut my face. After that, the rest of the bottles exploded as well. I left the bottles and glass in there, closed the lid and just ran the reaction anyway.

The smoke that came from the explosion smelled terrible, and the hydrogen-iodine gas made everything from the walls to the garage door glow with a purple tinge. Another girl who was staying at the house was already upset that we were there, and now she was really hostile. Here I was supposed to be this expert, and the first batch I tried to manufacture exploded in my face.

My bad luck with the bad equipment continued. There was only one cork for the flask, which had openings at the top and on the side. I decided to use my finger on the side opening. I put in the sodium hydroxide and swished it just a little bit. It shot like a volcano, blew the cork out and sprayed in my face.

I had to rinse my eyes out at the sink for more than an hour. They got so puffy that I couldn't see. When I finally tried to titrate the reaction again, it did the same exact thing. My eyes were so swollen shut that I couldn't see at all. Worse, I felt like an idiot.

I finally got it titrated and dried. The finished product was excellent, and that helped restore my reputation in Backlash's circle. The manufacturer of the Red Devil lye had changed the chemical makeup of the product, and I soon figured out that the explosive reaction had been created by the new lye I was using.

I was dividing my time between Pat's and Kelly's houses. Lloyd and I spent whatever I earned manufacturing playing video poker and gambling at Spirit Mountain Casino. Pat got out of jail, and Kelly's boyfriend got out right after that. Pat was upset that she was cut out of the action and kicked Artie and me out of the house at one in the morning. We couldn't go to Kelly's because her boyfriend didn't want us over there. Marianne was five months pregnant, and I didn't want her around the drugs. Furthermore, I'd started hooking up with Shannon, who'd broken up with Backlash. Since Shannon was living with Kelly, I couldn't stay with her.

Lloyd rented a room in the home of a couple, so we couldn't stay with him. In the middle of winter, all Artie and I had were our jackets. For two or three days, we literally lived on the streets. I stole some checks out of the garage of the place where Lloyd was staying. They were business checks from an exterminating business Lloyd and the guy he was renting the room from had once operated. Checks are good for about twenty dollars over the amount, so we could get a little cash as long as the checks lasted. We probably got a couple thousand from those bad checks.

Another manufacturing friend of Kelly's had a small house outside of Beaverton. He was on the run because the police had raided his home and found material for manufacturing drugs and making bombs. He wanted somebody to clean up the house and pay the rent. Kelly told me that if Artie and I were willing to do that, we could stay there.

The house was a dump inside and out. The guy who had lived there had been paranoid. All of the windows were covered with black plastic. There were no beds, only a reclining chair in the living room and a mattress on the floor of the bedroom. We stayed high and didn't sleep much. The power had been turned off, so Lloyd rented a generator in order for us to have electricity.

Almost attached to the house was another little house where an old hermit dude lived. He left maybe once a week and we seldom saw him. We started cleaning up and Lloyd helped me get money to manufacture more drugs. In the meantime, I got a vehicle from someone who owed Lloyd money. It was a 1977 International Scout, and was clearly stolen because the ignition was open—had to use a screwdriver to start the thing.

It was wintertime and freezing cold, and the generator sucked gas like you wouldn't believe. We'd have to siphon gas out of the Scout or call my dad and beg. I couldn't get it through my head to save money or buy gas, let alone food, in advance. Instead, I headed for the casino.

There were times Artie would say, "Maybe we should be smart this time and get something to eat."

And I'd say, "Screw you. If you don't want to play it my way, then get out of here."

He could only stand up to me for so long.

Although Kelly was nice, most of the new people in my life who manufactured were threatened by me because of how much I knew and how good my product was. I was probably more helpful than I needed to be, and some of them took offense to it. When you're on drugs, you think you know it all. I did, and so did they.

Pat got in trouble again, and that house went back to the owner. Kelly had skipped out on a court date, and she and her boyfriend left that house. The only person who was able to help me out was Lloyd. He offered to let Artie and me move out of the shack and into the house that Kelly had vacated.

I hadn't talked to Bobby J. for a while. I didn't want to ask him for money or let him know how far down I was. Once I had some product, I called him up. He hadn't seen the progression of how good my drugs had gotten.

"Wow," he said. "This is better than the stuff I've been selling."

He agreed to front me the money and gather the equipment and chemicals I needed to manufacture. I was back in the money again. The better drugs I had, the more connections I had, so there were now more options for me, and my life improved.

Once I had his support and a decent house, my self-esteem improved too, and I was more careful with the money. Before I headed for the casino, I made sure that I had everything I needed for the next run. I was far from perfect though. One time Bobby J. had given me three thousand dollars, and I didn't even get back to the house with it.

The infamous Uncle Rick

One day there was a knock at the door, and it was this guy of about fifty, not very tall, muscular but with a beer belly. He popped in through the front door with a bounce to his step.

"Where's Kelly?" he asked.

"She doesn't live here anymore," I told him.

"Well, who are you guys?"

"Who are you?" I asked.

"I'm Uncle Rick."

"Whose uncle?"

"That's just what they call me."

That was good enough for us. Soon we were talking about drugs and video poker.

"Oh," Uncle Rick said. "I'm an expert at video poker. I cash the machines out all the time with five thousand credits." That translated to twelve hundred fifty dollars. I was interested. "I just cashed out two machines," he said.

Soon I was saying, "Let's go play."

Uncle Rick had worked in scrap metal for years. Riding around with him was an experience.

"See that over there," he'd say.

"That air conditioner?" I asked.

"That thing's worth two hundred dollars."

The man had a metal detector in his head. I can't count the times I'd go with him in the middle of the night to pick up an air conditioner or other items he spied during the day.

Unlike the other manufacturers I knew, Uncle Rick was smart enough to take advice from me. He taught me about video poker, and I taught him about manufacturing.

Being on drugs made me feel one with the machines; it was like a pattern. Nine out of ten of the drug dealers and manufacturers I knew spent large amounts on video poker. I always bet the maximum credits, which was eight. Twenty dollars bought eighty credits. Any winning hand had the option of doubling up. An eight-credit win could turn into a five-hundred-twelve-dollar double up if you doubled up correctly eight times. I always liked to double up, but the way to really make the money with video poker is to double all the way. Uncle Rick's philosophy was double up until the machine wouldn't let you do it any more.

No one got between Uncle Rick and his video poker. One day we were at a bar down the street from his house—his favorite place to play, and every-one there knew him. All of the machines were taken, and a guy standing behind where we were playing leaned over to see how many credits we had, obviously wanting our machine. Uncle Rick warned the guy that he was crowding his space.

"How long are you going to be playing?" he asked, not taking the hint.

Uncle Rick kind of rotated in his chair and stood up. All in one motion, he punched the guy in the face, caught him, sat him on the ground and went back to playing video poker.

His friend the bartender came over and said, "You should have listened to him the first time" as he shoved the guy out the door.

Until then, I'd seen only Uncle Rick's cheerful side. He was one of those little guys who were tougher than they looked. It's always the big guys who brag about how bad they are, but obviously the guy who tried to crowd us wasn't the first one Uncle Rick had knocked out.

Looking back
Different people handle their addictions in a multitude of ways, but they're still addicts. Back then, I wished I was more like Uncle Rick. He knew when to say when, and I did not. He had house and a family, and I had neither. He could cash out two machines at video poker and go home, while I would be there all night. Maybe he was more comfortable in his addiction than I was with mine. Whenever I had down time, I thought about how lousy my life was and how much damage I had done. I needed to stay high to stay numb.

CHAPTER THIRTY-FOUR
METH BUST

I'll quit when it's not fun anymore. And I'm still having fun.
—Mikael Luman, back on speed

I'd usually take Artie with me when I played so that he could try to keep me from spending all my money. On this day in February, I was alone for some reason. I stopped at the first bar I went by and played video poker from early morning until seven at night. At the bar, I ran into a guy I'd known in my rave days. He invited me to a party at someone's house.

When I got back, Artie knew what I'd been doing but didn't say anything. I told him that I had to go somewhere, and I left. The reason I didn't invite him was that I knew there would be girls at the party, and he didn't feel right about my being with other girls since Marianne was pregnant.

I brought drugs to the party, and we partied hard. Marianne called all night, but I didn't answer. Finally, I passed out. One of the girls who was there heard my cell phone ringing and answered it. It was Marianne, and she was freaking out. The girl woke me up, but I was half in, half out of it. I took the phone and said, "Hello?" into the earpiece. She took the phone out of my hand, flipped it around and gave it back to me.

"Hello?" I said again.

"Where are you?" Marianne demanded.

"I don't know," I said, and at that moment, I didn't know.

"Well you'd better be at the house in forty-five minutes because I'm going over there."

I woke myself up and headed over to the house.

For security, I'd screwed a bracket onto the frame that covered the door. Marianne pulled up, and I was at the front door with a screwdriver so that I could unscrew the bracket, and she could come in.

She was almost nine months pregnant and furious with me. I needed to grab her and didn't want the screwdriver in my hand, so I tossed it into the kitchen. In slow motion, I watched it take a bounce and a hop, another little hop, and I knew where it was heading. The pointed end went right into the sliding glass door and shattered the whole thing. Just my luck. At least I was able to calm down Marianne, and she left.

I discovered that Lloyd was having an affair with the wife of the friend who was renting him a room. I knew that his living situation would have to change soon. Mine wasn't all that certain either. Remember, there was a broken window in the back of the house. We were manufacturing inside. It's really not a good idea to keep a house in those circumstances. I had a decent amount of product and chemicals and kind of had it together in terms of money.

In one of her tirades, Marianne had painted on one of the walls, and the landlord had given us a deadline on when we had to have the inside of the house repainted. There was also that purplish discoloration on the walls from the manufacturing. I knew it was time to do some painting. We put a piece of wood over the broken sliding glass door and were in the process of getting a new one.

Artie and I had left to play video poker that night. Lloyd called on my cell phone saying that his married girlfriend was working up the street. He wanted me to meet him at the house at ten p.m. to get some drugs so that they could get high before she had to go home. I told him the soonest I could be there was ten-fifteen.

At that time, Artie and I pulled up to the house. As we did, I spotted a police car about two blocks up the road with its lights off. When we pulled in, it came toward the house. I knew they were waiting for someone to pull in the driveway. I ran around the house to see if the board was up, knowing that if it was down, they would already be inside. It was down. I ran back around just as the police car was pulling up.

They started questioning us and put us in two separate cars. Artie knew that I was going to use my brother's name, and I knew the name he'd be giving them. It wasn't as though we weren't prepared for this possibility. As I sat there in the police car, I thought about what lousy timing it was. My son was supposed to be born in the next couple of days, and I was sure I'd be in jail when it happened.

They told me that they had gone into the house because the neighbors saw someone break in. When they got there, they saw a Corvette pulling out of the driveway and assumed someone had broken into the place. So, although it's questionable whether they should have gone inside, they did so. Then they went back out and called the narcotics team. I knew that the narcotics team was smart enough not to go in without a search warrant, but they were shining lights in the back.

After they finished questioning us, they let us go. They wouldn't let us take the Scout because we didn't have the registration. Again, I had no drugs, no chemicals, and I was getting tired of dragging Artie along with me. In order for me to find a place to go, I needed to break from him.

It was tough to do, but I finally said, "Hey, Artie. You need to go your way, and I need to go mine."

Starting over…again

I already had in my mind who I was going to call and where I was going to go. I'd run into Otis, his girlfriend, Cindy, and some of their friends a few days before. They were about four years younger than I and really impressed by my product. I called Otis because I knew that he'd had someone manufacture at his apartment before. When I told him what just happened, he agreed to drive me by the house so that I could see if the police officers were gone. But, there was an officer still posted outside. No way could I get inside and get back my stuff.

I didn't tell Otis and his group that the police had questioned me. When they came, I ran, I told them. I also made it sound as if I had pounds and pounds of supplies and a lot of cash in the house. I wanted them to think that I was more successful than I was so that they'd let me manufacture for them.

Otis helped me gather up everything that I needed, and he fronted the money. I ran my first reaction at his apartment. It was probably one of the best I'd ever done. There were four or five people over there when I finished, and they were extremely impressed.

Marianne called and said she thought she was having the baby. I gave Otis the product to sell and got a ride to Marianne's house. It was about ten p.m. and I was a little uncomfortable because Marianne's mom was there. I hadn't shaved and had been up for a while. I lay down with Marianne and fell asleep. Around four a.m., she said, "You need to get up."

I managed to do so, and we went to the hospital. Her dad was also there, and I fought to keep my eyes open. At about six that evening, they did an emergency c-section. I put on the scrubs and went into the operating room. About fifteen minutes later, they were handing me my son and I was able to give him his first bath.

My folks came down and visited with Marianne's parents. Marianne was resting.

Everyone was looking at me like, *What are you going to do now, Mikael?* And I was thinking, *What does it matter, since I'm going to be in jail for five years?* Full of shame and guilt, I felt like I was going to lose it. All I could think about was getting out of there and getting high.

Looking back

At some point, the fun is gone. It's not fun getting kidnapped, getting hit with a baseball bat, getting left somewhere and not having food to eat for five days. The longer you're around bad situations, the greater the chance of bad things happening to you. The down side about poor choices is that you end up having to live with the consequences. That's what happened to me.

CHAPTER THIRTY-FIVE
RUNNING OUT OF TIME

I can't stop now. If they catch me, I'm going to prison for a long time.
—Mikael Luman

I asked Marianne if I could use her car and told her I'd be back the next day. After I left, I met up with Bobby J. We got high and talked for a while. It was three days before I got the car back to Marianne. She and her parents were calling my cell phone. I couldn't deal with stepping back into that situation and facing it again.

Finally, I worked up the courage to take the car back. When I got to the hospital, Marianne's dad met me at the door and said we needed to talk. We went outside to the breezeway, and I knew what was coming. He demanded to know if I was ready to stand up and be a man. "What are your plans?" he asked.

Although he knew that I was a drug addict, I don't think he was aware that I was a meth manufacturer; Marianne had told them that I painted with my dad. I nodded, agreed with him and basically just let him talk.

Dealing with Marianne was worse than dealing with her dad. She said that she and my son were going to stay with her parents on the Oregon Coast for a month. In my mind, I figured that gave me a little time to get things figured out. I went back to Otis and Cindy's where I was staying and continued to manufacture. Once Marianne was gone, I was even less faithful than before. All I wanted to do was hook up with girls, make drugs and party.

One night I was playing video poker at Coaches, the bar I'd visited the night Artie and I had been pulled over. A cute blonde sat down next to me and started to play. When I was on speed, I could usually tell if other people were on it. It was especially easy when playing video poker. The blonde, although not as extreme as I was, had the movements and the mannerisms of someone who was high.

I looked over at her, and she kind of looked at me.

"Pretty good stuff?" I asked.

"Really good," she said.

"How good?"

"It's the best," she said.

"Better than this?" I pulled a clear container out of my pocket. Inside was the clearest, chunkiest crystal imaginable.

Her eyes widened. "That does look like some good stuff," she said.

We talked, and she told me her name was Wendy. Finally, she said there was somebody I should meet. That's how it is in the drug business. Everybody's always trying to hook up connections and build networks. She signaled for a guy to come over. His name was Sid. He was a big guy and bald—not mean looking but intimidating. On his right hand, he had only two fingers and a thumb.

Wendy mentioned that I had some good drugs. As it turned out, he was one of the biggest drug dealers in the area, and had a hand in everything from manufacturing to identity theft. I showed him the product and he said, "Wow. Can you get me some more of that and you and Wendy meet me over at my place?"

When we got to the house, we went into Sid's room. The rest of the house was kind of normal, but this room was full of computers and guns. We smoked the product, and he was impressed. "Why don't we team up?" he said.

I needed someone who was more level headed than I was when it came to the business, and Sid had lots of connections. He set me up with some ephedrine, and I continued to hook up him and Wendy with drugs. Sid was more the get-high-and-get-down-to-business type. He was facing charges, too, so he had to spend time with his attorney.

Overdid it

One day he called me and asked me to come over. By the time I got to his house, I was so high from drinking liquefied crystal that I couldn't even walk without shaking. He asked, "What happened to you?" and I tried to tell him while still twitching.

"I just want to lie down," I said.

"No," he said. "You're coming with me."

We got in his Jeep and drove over to Safeway, and I started getting leg cramps. I ended up on the floor in the store, twitching and rubbing my legs. He helped me up, and we went to pick up a computer at a shop where he was having it repaired. He left the computer with me, and we agreed to get together the next day.

We never did. The next day I got a call from Wendy. Sid was dead—shot himself in the head. His death hit the people in his group really hard, and rumors about how it happened flew. A couple of days later I talked to the girl who had been in the room when he blew his brains out.

"What really happened?" I asked.

She couldn't speak without crying. "He put one bullet in the gun, spun the chamber, put the gun to his head and fired. It's not like what you see on TV. It's real blood and real brains and a real hole in someone's head." She was horrified by what she'd witnessed, and I doubt that she will ever recover from it.

Some said it was suicide; others said it was an accident. Sid's mother had committed suicide when he was eight. His dad had died right after that. Yet on the outside, he looked as if he had his act under control and was stable. The bottom line is that Russian Roulette or not, putting a gun to your head is suicide. So is drug addiction. Every time you use, it's a potential suicide.

Looking back

When my son was born, I had no emotion left in me. Drugs take away your pain but they take away your ability to care. Life, death, love, even fatherhood were just words to me. All I wanted to do was to get high, but I didn't know how much longer that was going to be able to last. The walls were coming down around me.

CHAPTER THIRTY-SIX
GRAB AND RUN

I think that I can get whatever I want.
I am a manipulator and can use any mask.
—Mikael Luman, Personal Insight Statement
Oregon SUMMIT Program

Wendy introduced me to her friend Kristen who worked at a deli with video poker machines, which were its main source of income. The deli had about twenty locations throughout Portland and earned a lot of money. Kristen told me that the poker machines brought in about twenty thousand dollars per deli on a Friday night. Then, she explained the process of how they collected the money.

A van would pull up in front of the store. The driver would roll in a cooler with cigarettes for the day and a few other items that needed to be dropped off. Then, he'd take out the garbage, replace the surveillance tape from the day before with a new one, and wheel out the previous day's cooler full of money. Each van had five or six locations on its route.

"If you were just to come in with a cooler and a dolly, I'd pretend you were a driver and let you take the cooler with the money," she said. My criminal brain jumped into gear.

The conversation took place on a Friday. I planned to do it the next morning. The driver usually came around nine a.m., and I needed to get there right before the real driver. Her plan was to tell him that the driver had just left five minutes before.

Saturday morning I was at Wendy's house. This was the first and only time that Wendy and I had gotten together. Obviously, I wasn't thinking about going to the deli. I missed the opportunity that day.

The next morning at about seven-thirty, I was buying a dolly and a cooler, borrowing a truck. I arrived at the deli, wheeled in the cooler, changed the videotape, grabbed the cooler and left. Back at Otis', I was counting the money—about eight thousand dollars. Kristen called, crying, and said that she got scared and hadn't said anything when the new driver came. He'd just picked up the cooler and left, and she didn't know what to do. Now she was going to be implicated for not saying there had been a first driver there.

"What are we going to do?" she said.

My plan was to find the van on its route and steal the contents of the other coolers. They wouldn't know which cooler had been hit first, and I'd have that much more money. I had Otis' car and needed to find a getaway driver. So I called Jack, a guy I thought would help me—not the most reliable guy, but I thought I had no other option.

I picked him up and followed the route Kristen had given me. We caught up with the van at the third-to-last stop. After he brought out the garbage was when I was going to go in, empty the coolers and run, but I needed something to carry the money with. I went into a nearby sporting goods store and bought a backpack.

We followed the van to the next-to-last stop, and the driver started the usual routine. With the positioning of the van and the availability of escape, I knew this was the time to act.

"Jack," I said. "Park right here, with the car facing that direction, the door open and be ready to drive when I come running."

I didn't want to take the risk, but I felt I had to. I walked down to the van scoping out the situation as I went. I opened the side van door—relieved to find it unlocked, half-expecting to have to break in—opened the coolers, removed the money bags and stuffed them into the backpack. As I was taking the last one, I saw the driver running out of the store.

I ran to where my "getaway driver" was. He was parked the wrong way, the door wasn't open and he was talking on a cell phone. I smacked the hood of the car—shocked the guy was this stupid—and signaled for him to follow me. Then I cut back behind the strip mall.

When I got to the next main street, out of the corner of my eye, I saw a white Bronco. It turned and tried to hit me. I did a spin and continued to run. The Bronco accelerated and knocked me over. While scrambling to get up, the two guys in the Bronco decided to be heroes, got out of it and started beating me.

The next think I knew, an off-duty police officer put me in thumb cuffs. The guys were yelling and screaming. I didn't know where my getaway driver was.

The police showed up, and I told them I needed an ambulance. They transported me to the hospital. Again, I used my brother's name, knowing that at least that would give me a slight chance of being able to make bail and getting out. I was handcuffed to the bed of the hospital room. The nurse was a guy who I ran track with in high school.

"You're Jeremy Luman?" he said with a confused look.

"Yeah, I'm Jeremy," I said.

"So how's your brother doing?" he asked. "You know, you look so much like Mikael."

The police were right there, and I couldn't believe I'd get away with pretending to be my brother. Finally, they checked me out and felt that I was fine to go to jail. The fingerprinting system at the jail was computerized. It could take a day or two before they could match fingerprints and find out who I really was.

All of the phones in the jail are recorded. I called Otis' and said, "Jeremy Luman, Washington County, two thousand five hundred dollars," and hung up the phone.

They had half the money that I'd gotten from the cooler the first time, and I hoped that they'd understand my cryptic message. About four hours later, Jeremy Luman's name was called, and I went down to sign the release material. Otis and Cindy were waiting for me in the parking lot.

The police found a card in my back pocket that had Kristen's name and phone number on it. In the meantime, she'd called them and said that someone stole the money from the deli where she worked. They ultimately figured out that she had something to do with the missing money.

The fingerprints came back as Mikael Luman and not Jeremy, as I'd told them. Then they listened to the phone recordings in the jail. According to the police reports, I called four times but got through only once. They found out that it was Otis I called, so they went over to his house. He was working on his car when they arrived. They started questioning him about the incident and mentioned my name. After searching the apartment for me, they read Otis and Cindy their rights and charged them with being accessories because they knew that I was Mikael Luman. It was similar to when my dad was arrested; they were using the charges against Otis and Cindy to get to me.

The police asked where I was, and they said that I'd left the night that they bailed me out. That was true. I knew that it was only a matter of time before they'd trace me to Otis'.

Marianne had gotten back into town and was upset that I hadn't been to see her or my son. She'd picked me up at Otis' and Cindy's and taken me back to her apartment. I stayed with her for a couple of days trying to figure out what I was going to do. Kristen was in trouble as well. I was trying to find a place for us that was away from the group that I'd been with. People to whom I owed money were looking for me, and so were the police.

Lousy protection

Lenny, an older guy, was a dealer I'd met who was trying to learn how to manufacture. Bald with a leather vest, he looked the rebel outlaw part better than he lived it. I called him, and Kristen and I stayed a few days at his apartment while I gave him tips on how to improve his manufacturing.

It's amazing how small the world is. I was thinking that I was in a safe place. The third day we were there, Ren—Brody's girlfriend who'd tried to rip me off and run over me in her van—showed up. Until the ripoff/van incident, I'd thought I could trust her. Since then, I didn't. She was there for only a few minutes and left. I knew it was time for me to get out of there. I told Lenny I was leaving.

"Oh, you got nothing to worry about, man," he said. "I'll protect you."

I walked outside, needing to get away. A van was parked around the corner, and I sensed danger. A few seconds after I went back inside, the front door was kicked open. A guy with a gun burst in and started beating me up. He kicked me and punched me in the face and stomach.

Lenny, the tough-guy dude, stood in the hall, saying, "Hey, man, respect my house, okay."

"Stand up," the guy demanded, and I did my best.

Then a guy I owed money to came in. His name was Clifford, and I'd met him through Andre—a friend of crazy stalker Holly's—when I was still trying to learn how to manufacture. He'd given us fifteen hundred dollars for ephedrine. Andre also had a bad video poker habit, and that was what happened to the money. Instead of telling Clifford the truth, Andre blamed me. Now, I had to pay the price.

"Where's my fifteen hundred dollars?" Clifford demanded.

"Did you ask your best friend, Andre?" I said.

Then I told him the story.

He was angrier about Andre lying to him than he was about the money. He punched me a couple of times for good measure, and then they left. Lenny just stood there, watching it happen.

"Dude," I said. "Why didn't you do something? Why'd you just stand there?"

Instead of answering, he went to his room. There are people who are doers under pressure, and those who are not. I think he just froze.

Kristen and two other girls came out of the bedroom. "Gosh," Kristen said. "I can't believe that Lenny didn't help you."

She wasn't the only one. Lenny had only talked protection, but I could no longer count on him. I knew I couldn't afford to worry about anyone but myself. I told Kristen that, and she understood. My options were getting fewer and fewer.

Evan, a dealer who'd bought from me, knew a couple of girls in Lake Oswego who had a place where I could stay. Linda, the girl whose parents owned the house, was really cute, which motivated me even more to hide out there. I hooked up with her and stayed there about a month and a half. While there, I continued to manufacture, and I cut ties with the whole Otis-and-Cindy crowd.

Every so often, I thought about Marianne and my son and felt bad that I was being such an absent father. I tried to call her. I was in a low place and wanted to see her and my son. Her cell phone number was no longer in operation and she'd moved from her apartment. I drove by places where she had worked, but I could find no sign of her. Marianne had successfully removed herself from my life.

Looking back

You can't run forever from the police or from the people you rip off. The people who love you will put up with your lifestyle for only so long. At this point, I was just trying to stay alive and out of jail. I was too far in to even fathom how to get out.

CHAPTER THIRTY-SEVEN
DEAD END

I lie any time I feel it will benefit me. I tell people what they want to hear in order to get what I want. I give false information when questioned by the police. I even lie to myself, convincing myself that what I am doing is not wrong. I do whatever I want, however I want, whenever I want.
—Mikael Luman, Personal Accountability Statement
Oregon SUMMIT Program

In Lake Oswego, my life was pretty low-key and fairly comfortable because Linda was there. I had drugs, I had a girl, and I had Evan—who was able to go out and round up everything I needed to manufacture. I always found a way to ruin a relationship with a girl or a partner in drugs, and this time I did both.

Evan brought a DJ into town from Seattle, and the plan was for me to manufacture a huge batch for the DJ to take back. With manufacturing, a lot can go wrong, and that's what happened in this case. I failed to extract as much ephedrine as I'd expected. We were at Linda's, and I was under pressure. Instead of testing just a little amount, I was rushed and tested the whole thing. As a result, I messed up and didn't get the amount we wanted. Evan started yelling at me, and I tackled him. I didn't get upset very often, but I'd had enough.

He left, and that was the end of our association. At the same time, my relationship with Linda was in trouble. I had just started hanging out with Randy, a dealer who lived in St. Helens, which was forty-five minutes from Lake Oswego. Through him, I got reacquainted with Carla, who I'd lusted after back when I'd had the party pad. At a party, I told Linda I didn't want to be with her anymore, and she left crying. I borrowed four thousand dollars to manufacture from another dealer, but instead, I took everyone to the casino. Once again, I lost it all and came back empty handed.

A day or two later, Randy and I went over to Carla's friend's house to sell her drugs. The friend, Brandy, said that she needed to run up the street about fifteen blocks and drop something off to some guy she knew and asked us to go with her. The dude was pretty sketched out but seemed harmless. We chatted for a little bit, and then Brandy, Carla, Randy and I took off to head back to Brandy's house.

When we arrived, I gave Randy the signal that I was going to go into the room with Carla and do what we had been waiting to do since we'd reconnected. When we left the bedroom a couple of hours later, Randy and Brandy were gone. A few minutes later, Randy walked in. No more than thirty seconds after that, we heard a screaming woman, and in ran Brandy. Right behind her, an ax hit the door and slid across the floor. In ran the tweeker dude from earlier that morning, yelling about her stealing something from him.

I grabbed the ax so that it couldn't be used as a weapon anymore. Randy tackled the tweeker to the ground and started to choke him out. He continued to yell and scream about being ripped off. When he finally calmed down, Randy let him go, and he left without his ax, still muttering. I followed him to the door and made sure he wasn't waiting outside. *How did this guy walk fifteen blocks with an ax in his hand without anybody noticing?* I wondered. But just then I spotted a police car a block up the street—the last thing I wanted to see being on the run. The car moved toward the house. Obviously someone had noticed the ax and called the cops.

"Randy," I said, "You guys go out and explain to the police officer what happened. I'll hide in the bedroom."

I was scared to death and would have gone out the back window if I hadn't feared they'd mistake me for the ax guy. Randy and the girls went outside for what seemed like an eternity. Then Brandy came back inside.

I whispered her name, but she must have forgotten that I was hiding in the house because she started screaming and yelling, "He's in here."

I guess having someone come after her with an ax earlier, not to mention the crystal she'd smoked, made her a little paranoid. Carla calmed her down, and the police officer left. I thought for sure they were going to come into the house, guns drawn, thinking I was the ax man.

I sent Randy over to Linda's to get my manufacturing equipment, and the only place left for me to stay was his house in St. Helens. His girlfriend also stayed there, but she wasn't into drugs or to having me around. Randy, like the other people I'd stayed with, thought he'd benefit by having me there. He had a garage off the house where he wanted me to manufacture.

In Portland, there are so many crazy people and so much crazy stuff going on, that the drug addicts just blend in with the rest of the weirdoes. In St. Helens, we stood out. There are more police per capita there than any other place in Oregon. Since Randy had a house there, he was already under suspicion. I wouldn't even let him talk on his cell phone when he was driving at night.

I was running a batch at Randy's house when a house up the street was raided by the police. Even though the reaction was running in the pressure cooker, I told Randy, "I'm out of here."

He didn't want me to go and accused me of being paranoid, which I was—extremely. But then I spotted someone watching the house.

"Look at that," I said. "Still think I'm paranoid?"

Finally, he agreed that I should leave. He called Thomas, a low-key guy who lived with his mom out in the woods. I didn't want to stay with a guy and his mother, but she was cool with it, and I had no choice. I was convinced the cops would be at Randy's any minute. I finished the reaction there, but I didn't want to stay because Thomas and his mother were moving. The next day Randy was arrested. So much for paranoia.

One last time

Wayne was an older guy who worked at the cabinet shop. I'd met him when Randy and I had gone to his house to sell him drugs, and we'd hit it off. I asked Thomas if he would give me a ride to Wayne's, and I was hoping that Wayne would let me stay there.

Although he had a lot of people in and out of the house, he went to work regularly and kept his yard and garden in impeccable shape. The house was clean and picked up, and Wayne got along with his landlord. He was always outside mowing the lawn. It was a more comfortable environment than I'd been used to for some time, and the focus wasn't entirely drugs. Still, I couldn't really relax there.

I had a bunch of Wayne's friends do the legwork for me, and I manufactured in his garage. I'd been there a little more than a month when it happened. I'd had another one of my bad feelings, and Wayne and I had discussed moving everything to the home of a friend of his.

Dawn, a good-looking friend of Wayne's who liked to hang out at his house, had a boyfriend in jail. The boyfriend didn't like it because he knew

Dawn was doing drugs. While he was in jail, he found out that manufacturing was going on at the house, and he snitched.

I had just finished a batch and put most of it in the refrigerator to start crystallizing. On the screen of one of the monitors of our surveillance cameras, I saw a van pulling into the driveway. I ran out into the front room, looked out the back window and spotted flashing lights in the field. Just then, I heard three loud bangs on the back door, and someone shouted, "Police! Search warrant!"

I charged through the front door, shoulder down, expecting to have to force my way through multiple cops, but there was no one there. Since my weight was forward and there was no one to hit, I fell, bounced off the porch and slid on the grass—still wet from a recent storm. I crawled to the fence, scurried over it, dropped down and ran to Highway 30.

From there, I crossed the highway, where there was a nursery; it was dark, and my path was littered with potted plants. Although it was only a couple hundred yards long, it took what seemed like forever. I scrambled through them, falling repeatedly. Figuring I was pursued by police dogs, I jumped into a creek, thinking it would throw them off my trail. Then, I got out and followed the train tracks about a half-mile, where I knew another friend lived. His house was on the highway, and I climbed though a lot of prickly blackberry bushes to get there.

The flashing lights lit up the sky. There had to be at least ten police cars. I got a change of clothes, and a woman who lived in the trailer park next door drove me to a cute girl's house I'd met through Randy. Although she sometimes used drugs, she worked at a dentist's office, had a daughter and was fairly responsible. Even though she dated a guy who was a dealer, I figured it was a fairly safe place to go. I stayed there that night. If I'd been smart, I would have gotten out of Dodge, but I was just tired.

Twelve days later, I returned to her place and crashed, out of drugs, out of money, out of energy—unaware that her jealous boyfriend would call the police.

I was sleeping when they arrived, vaguely aware of voices, but unable to wake up. The next thing I knew, three of them were standing around the bed, and I was handcuffed.

Looking back

Right before I was arrested, I had a feeling that something was wrong. In the past, I would have run, but I didn't have any run left in me. I'd hung around that town for days after the house had been raided, and looking back, I believe that I was waiting for the inevitable. Even as I was arrested, I was relieved that this chapter of my life was over, that I was still alive. I realize now that the emotion I felt was hope. Whatever happened to me next, I was going to make the best of it.

CHAPTER THIRTY-EIGHT
SPECIAL CALLING

I think that you believe in God. I know that you once did. If you still do, you must know that He is much more tolerant and understanding than any of us give Him credit for. He wanted us to come here in order to have experiences, and learn from our experiences that we should avoid the bad and prize the good. You also have friends who, along with your family, would do anything to help you.
—Steve Dalton, church leader

There were four bunks and about eighteen of us in the room, most of us sleeping on mattresses. If I had been sober, it would have been awful, but now I was coming down off a high and all I wanted was a place to sleep—even if it was in jail. I vaguely remembered being interrogated by the police and asking for one last cigarette before they took me in.

Columbia County is even smaller than Washington County, especially the drug community. The jail was so small that the sergeant would still come in and cook breakfast for everybody, and I knew a couple of the guys in my cell from my dealings. The guy who turned me in was in the next group cell. "Is Luman over there?" he and his buddies would yell through the bars. "Are you Luman?" they'd shout as I walked by.

A couple of weeks passed, and I finally called my parents. Obviously, they weren't that receptive, but they finally agreed to get me an attorney. My parents said that Marianne had been in the hospital and had almost died from spinal meningitis. I called her to apologize for what I'd done. Although she was still angry with me, she said it was okay for me to call her again.

At that point, I was still thinking that I could get the charges dropped.

179

After two or three weeks, I decided that I wanted to change and stop doing drugs, but my actions hadn't changed. I was top dog in there, and everyone had questions for me about manufacturing. My popularity was more important to me than my desire to change, and I spent a lot of my time talking to them about drugs.

Stand up

From as far back as I can remember, long before I started using drugs, I always used humor as a way to gain acceptance, feel better about myself or be popular. Most of the time, it was at the expense of other people. There could be eight people in the room, and I would pick on one of them to be the brunt of my jokes.

My stand-up routines followed me into prison. Many of the stories I've recounted in this book were part of the stand-up routine, although I would use the funny version instead of the honest one. The material focused on sex, women, drugs and money. I could do more than an hour on Holly—the crazy stalker woman. I drew laughs when I explained about the seven different types of women and how to get each type into bed. I used Dee a lot; I couldn't have invented anyone more outrageous.

The woman who worked at the control station at night monitored our conversations.

"Hey, Luman," she said one night. "You need to get into your bunk."

"Can you give me a minute?" I said. "I'm in the middle of a routine right now."

"What routine?"

"Listen to it for just a few minutes," I said. "And if it isn't any good, you can tell me to get back in my bunk."

After a few minutes, she started laughing. From then on, it became a nightly ritual. I wouldn't even know she was there until I could hear her laughter.

"I knew you were listening," I'd say.

After about three months, we moved into the new jail, where we had two-man cells and a common area in the middle. After being there for a month or so, I got transferred into the trustee tank. My first job was laundry. I'd put on about forty pounds, and I was looking fat. I decided that I was going to fold more laundry than anyone in the history of the jail. I was so sore the next day that I could barely move my arms.

I was upgraded to the kitchen. My parents had sent me my scriptures from church, and I'd started reading and praying a little. At first, it was difficult to facilitate a change because I was in a criminal environment. The trustee tank was a dorm, and I couldn't read the Bible without everyone noticing.

A guy who was supposed to be a pedophile came into the dorm. One night before dinner, I wrote on a piece of paper, "Get on your tricycle and pedophile your way out of here," and left it at the place where he always sat for dinner. When he started to sit down, he read it and started yelling about who did it.

"I wrote it," I said. "You have a problem with that?"

We fought, and the guards came in, separated us and took us to isolation cells. I guess I wanted to look tough or impress the other guys, but that incident was the changing point for me. After three or four days in the isolation cell, I felt really bad. The guy was in another cell, and I apologized to him. I realized that I was not being the person I wanted to be.

The changing process

I decided I wanted to change and the first thing I addressed was my image. At lunch, we got out of our cells for three hours. I borrowed a pair of shoes from a fellow inmate who had a doctor's approval, and at lunchtime, I would run up and down the twenty steps that led to the second tier of cells.

The first time I did it, I could go up and down only ten times. The first week I ran up and down the stairs three hundred and fifty times. I'd do push-ups and sit-ups in my cell at night. Between sets, I read my scriptures and Norman Vincent Peale's *The Power of Positive Thinking*, which I found on the book rack.

I started noticing in conversations that I was swearing all of the time. My new goal was to recognize when I did so and ultimately to stop myself before I swore. At night, I started writing down all of the things I did that day that I needed to repent for and that I wanted to change. I prayed for forgiveness, guidance and help. I was also praying that I'd get out of jail, but as I was to learn, what we think is best for us is not always the case.

28 February 2001
Mikael Luman
C/o Columbia County Jail
St. Helens, OR 97051

Dear Mikael,
I am so happy that you have accepted your "fate" and

decided that it is time to make a change in your life. If you are truly repentant, the power of the atonement will make you a new person. However, everything comes with a price. You will need to pay for your "sins" before you will be free of them. Let the atonement work for you and know that if you are truly repentant, all will work out for you, your son and Marianne.

I love you, Mikael. I look forward to running Hood to Coast and doing other things together. In fact, I think it would be great to run as a three-generation team someday with you and my grandson.

Love,
Dad

I'd always known that I had a special calling. That was part of the reason for the guilt I'd experienced when I was using drugs. Now, I realized that my calling, although I hadn't refined it, would involve helping young people avoid making the mistakes that I had. I thought of it as A Generation Free, and my slogan was: "All things are possible if you are free." Now I had a mission, and I knew that I was in prison for a reason. I'd experienced everything I had so that I could end up in that cell making the decisions and plans I was making right then.

I continued running the stairs. The second week I ran up and down six hundred and ninety-five times. The more stairs I was running, the more I was reading at night, the more sit-ups I was doing and the more I was getting into my calling. Two months later, I'd gone from two hundred four pounds to one seventy-eight. I did one thousand four hundred forty-four pushups, thirteen thousand, six hundred crunches and went up and down the stairs nineteen hundred times. My record for two hours and fifty minutes on the stairs was six hundred and fifty times.

I'd always regretted not giving a hundred and ten percent to practicing when I was in school. Yet in prison, there was no one telling me that I needed to be running the stairs or that I needed to run harder the first hour or hour and a half. The glory's always at the end and it's the first ninety percent of the journey that's the hard part. If you want the true glory, you've got to put in the first ninety percent. I learned that on the stairs, and I got back my hope and faith in myself. I was proving to myself every day what I could accomplish, not just in athletics, but in life.

Everyone in the cell got involved. Some refilled my water. New people coming in would ask, "How long is that guy going to run the stairs?"

"The whole lunch break," they would say.

And of course, they were happy to relieve me of the lunch I gave away every day. I'd been in jail for eight months when the guy who'd held me accountable was moved to my pod. In jail, a rat is still a rat, and you've got a legitimate beef with him. When the guy came into the cell, everybody thought that I was going to react the way that they would have reacted—which would have been starting a fight and getting into it with him. I'm sure he was expecting the same thing. It was a pretty big deal, and everyone was waiting to see how it played out.

I wanted to get it over with and move on. I walked up to him, and he was pretty defensive. "I don't have a problem with you," I said. "I don't have a problem with what you did because it's gotten me to where I am now."

I had already gotten over the fact that he turned me in. I wanted him to know that I appreciated the fact that I was able to change my life, and that he was the one, regardless of his motives, who started that process.

He explained why he did it. He had a son, and he was upset that his wife was over at Wayne's house getting high while he was in jail. I could see his point of view, and after that we got along fine. People around you notice change taking place, even in prison. With me, it revolved around the stairs and losing weight. I was becoming a different person, and the people around me could see that. Instead of talking about drugs, sex and manufacturing, I started talking about my desire to change. It takes only one person in a group feeling that way to affect everyone in the group.

When I was doing the stand-up, I was "closet changing." I was reading the Bible in private, wanting to be different but not acting different. I was doing the same things that I'd done as a kid when I'd wanted to fit in and be popular—never standing up for what I believed in. That behavior had led to nothing but trouble in the past; it was what had fueled my addictions. Every addict has that feeling of guilt or shame they're trying cover up or hide from. This was how I covered mine.

I'd always heard, "Lead by example." Finally, I could start to see that through my own change, I could start the process of change in other people. My desire to help others was stronger than ever. Two months after that, the new day sergeant informed me that he had decided I could no longer continue my stair runs. That was all right. I was focused. I had my discipline back. I was at peace.

Looking back

Nothing that happened to me was as bad as I imagined it was going to be. I had always thought the worst. Jail is only bad because it keeps you from doing what you want to do. Even it can be a good tool if you take advantage of it. I'd been in jail before, but this time I was ready to use it as an opportunity to change and to focus on my calling.

CHAPTER THIRTY-NINE
A NEW PURPOSE

*This certifies that Mikael Luman, Aug. 13, 2002, has successfully com-
pleted participation in the Oregon SUMMIT Program; the
Department of Correction's intense six-month program of discipline,
education, cognitive change and substance abuse education.*
—Certificate of completion, 2002

I had charges in Columbia County for manufacturing, distribution and
possession. I had charges in Clackamas County for a probation violation. In
Washington, I had charges for manufacturing, distribution, possession,
perjury, robbery and burglary. After about nine months, my attorney got the
Clackamas charge dropped with credit for the time I'd already served.

I went to court in Columbia County, and the judge sentenced me to
fifty-three months but said I was eligible for the prison boot camp program. In
Washington County, I was sentenced to forty-eight months that ran concurrent
with the fifty-three I received from Columbia. Up until that time, I'd been held in
county jails. After that, I was shipped to the prison intake center and to a mini-
mum-security prison. Although the odds of getting into the boot camp program
right away were not good, I was accepted after five weeks of being in prison.

The boot camp was on the Oregon coast, up on a hill—a former military
site. It was a six-month program that would allow me to cut years off my
sentence. Of the seventy-five people who get accepted, thirty-five percent
graduate. Once you're kicked out of the boot camp program, you aren't
eligible to return. The first day, we were all given buzz cuts.

There were women in the program as well as men but talking to or even looking at the women was an automatic ticket out of the program. That was really difficult for me. I always liked to talk and be funny, and I had a tough time keeping my mouth shut. But I'd already made the decision that I wanted to change and boot camp was the way to get me there sooner.

It also gave me a lot of structure. Everything was on a schedule and the day started at five-thirty a.m. We had five minutes to be shaved, dressed and ready to go out for physical training. After breakfast, we'd either go on work crews or to classes. The classes consisted of path finders, cognitive thinking and twelve-step material.

Within the first couple of weeks, we were asked by the community officers to explain what we were in there for. Most of the other people were first- or second-time offenders. A high percentage of the inmates were in for drug-related crimes. One guy, Travis, was in for vehicular manslaughter. In his mid-thirties, he was a blond, slender guy who had gotten drunk and made the decision to drive. It had been the first time he'd ever driven drunk, he said, and I believed him. He'd run a red light, hit a car and killed three people. He couldn't talk about it without crying.

I felt that I could have been in the same situation that he was. Anyone who does drugs or drinks and drives could have that happen to them. Travis could have very easily been in prison for twenty-five years, but his real punishment turned out to be living with the guilt and the shame of what he'd done.

Roy, another guy in there, was also Christian. He was a football player, married and didn't use drugs. When playing golf, he'd gotten into an argument with a guy, punched him in the face and broken his jaw in six places, and was in for assault.

We were allowed visitors for two hours every other Sunday. My dad drove almost eight hours round trip each time from Portland—he never missed a Sunday. Marianne lives on the Oregon Coast with her parents and my son, who was two. She visited sometimes as well and brought my son to see me. Then, I thought we'd get back together. It seemed like the right thing to do. I wanted to make things right.

Old habits die hard

Five weeks prior to graduation, my grandmother died, and I needed to call Marianne to ask her if she'd come to the funeral with me. The phone monitor, Bronson, was in another room, and since we were not allowed to go into each other's rooms, I shouted for him to come out.

"Bronson, come out here, please. I need to talk to you."

He shook his head, laughing, and then reluctantly came out.

That piqued my interest. "What's going on in there?" I asked.

"You're not going to believe this," he said. "We about have Becker convinced to put muscle rub on his jock itch." I no longer cared that I wasn't supposed to be in the room.

Becker was one of those guys who liked to be in the limelight. He probably knew that the guys were putting him on, but he also probably had no idea what a dumb move he was about to make.

"My dad's a doctor, and that's what he recommends," one of the guys told him

"I'm an athlete," I said. "I use it all the time." He took a little scoop, and I said, "No, Becker. You'd better take a big scoop if you want it to work."

Soon he was screaming, hanging onto and shaking the bunk, crying like a dying animal.

I ran out into the open area, laughing so hard that I couldn't talk. Everyone came running out. I lay down on the ground, doubled up with laughter. Becker went into take a hot shower, which made it even worse. He screamed for at least twenty minutes. The community officer was furious. She demanded to know who was in the room. All of us who had been said so. It was just another reminder of the kind of person I didn't want to be. I should have told Becker not to put on the muscle rub, but instead I was the one who told him to put on more.

The next day was a Saturday, my grandmother's funeral. My dad picked me up in the morning, and Marianne met us at the boot camp gate. It was pretty emotional for me. My grandmother's death had been sudden, and I'd never had a chance to tell her that I was committed to changing. Before we left, I asked my dad to stop the car, and I went back to the grave and promised my grandmother that I would follow through with my special calling, and that I was ready to step up and fulfill that.

On Monday, when we were in class, they called for four of us to go to the counselor's office. The head of the program was extremely strict. I thought for sure that I was heading back to prison. There were three weeks left. It was hard for me to believe that I'd do something that stupid that close to getting out. We were down to thirty-one of the original seventy-five people. The four of us were in the top of the group in terms of evaluations, and the counselor, Mrs. Allen, liked all of us.

"I don't know if I can keep you guys from being kicked out," she said. "I've been begging and pleading, but it doesn't look good."

When we got in the superintendent's office, there was a lot of swearing going on.

"Did you guys think that was funny?" he demanded. And when we answered in the negative, he said, "Then why did you do it? If it hadn't been for Mrs. Allen standing up for you, you'd be out of the program."

Instead of being kicked out, we were recycled. I didn't get to graduate with my group. My poor decision had cost me two months. It was more difficult the second time than it had been the first, and they were a lot harder on me. Of the four of us who got recycled, only two of us graduated.

My parents, Marianne and my son attended the graduation. We did a marching formation, took our seats, and the superintendent gave a speech about the program and how people had been helped by it. Travis, who'd killed three people when he'd driven drunk, received one of the best evaluations. He spoke at the graduation and broke down and cried then, too, as he talked about how he'd always have to live with what he'd done. Most of the audience was in tears as well.

Transition Leave

After graduation, we were on short leashes and had ninety days where we could still be sent back to prison if we did anything wrong. I had to report to my probation officer every day. I also had to have permission to leave Washington County. They gave me a two-week deadline to get a job. I was lucky that I could stay with my parents and that a close family friend employed me to do finish carpentry. For others, it was a struggle to get and keep employment, and some had to stay at Oxford House—a group home.

After being separated from society for twenty-four months, it was a struggle for me to stay away from activities that would lead me to trouble. I was concerned that I'd run into old friends at the probation office or even at AA/NA meetings or the grocery store. There was always that fear of having to go back and finish my sentence. I had to attend three classes and three Alcoholics Anonymous or Narcotics Anonymous meetings a week.

I got my driver's license in December, and that made it easier for me to drive to see Marianne and my son. My relationship with Marianne was always a struggle, but I still felt I wanted to salvage it. I also needed to see my son and to gain the trust of Marianne and her parents.

When I first got out of boot camp, all I could think about was starting a nonprofit organization. I started biking and running, the same way that I did the stairs—each day trying to do more than I had the day before. Looking back, I don't think it was the right time in my life to try to start the nonprofit—I had no credibility and I hadn't been in recovery long enough to deal with my own demons. I wanted it to be easy, to just get out of boot camp, put out a flier, start a nonprofit and go around collecting money. Knee surgery ultimately interfered with my plans, and I can see now that it was for the best.

After my job as a finish carpenter was over, I worked in an auto dealership. Although I always thought selling cars would be fun, it wasn't the best place for a recovering addict. There were too many people there using. They didn't influence me, but they weren't the kind of people I wanted to be hanging out with, either.

A job opened up at a mortgage company where my father worked. Although I could not be a loan officer because of my criminal record, I was able to work in the leasing department. When I was hired there, I felt I had something to prove. I worked twelve hours a day, which was good for me because I was trying to replace old habits. I felt I'd been given an opportunity and wanted to prove that it was something that I could do.

Right woman/wrong woman

I always tell people that you might not necessarily know that it's the right person, but you know when it's the wrong one. That was what happened with Marianne. She was still angry with me about how I'd hurt her before I'd been arrested, and I don't blame her. Life with her was like walking on broken glass. I'd had that with Dee, and I didn't want my life to be like that any more. I just wasn't willing to make that sacrifice.

I knew what I wanted to do with my life, and I needed somebody who would be supportive of my plans for a nonprofit organization and my commitment to helping people. With Marianne, I didn't feel I was ever going to be able to do that. When I talked to her about my plans, she acted as if they were a pipe dream. I couldn't blame her; she'd witnessed enough of my pipe dreams during our relationship. Even though she had every right to feel that way, I knew that I'd changed, and I needed a woman who believed in me.

Because I was afraid of how she'd react if I broke it off, I started dating behind her back. When you're trying to be clean, where do you find girls? In the past, I met them at parties and clubs. Now, I felt the safest way to do it was online. I posted my profile and photo on Internet sites. On a Christian site, I spotted a photo of a beautiful redhead who lived in Utah. Her name was Amanda. I contacted her, we talked, and a week later, we met in Ontario—the halfway point between our two cities. On the night we met in person, I told her the truth about my past. I thought that was easier than waiting. If it was going to be an issue, then she wasn't the type of person I wanted to be with anyway.

Within a week of meeting Amanda, I erased all of the numbers in my cell phone address book. Although I told Amanda about Marianne, I didn't tell Marianne about her. Marianne found out, of course, and was upset. I helped her move back to Oregon Coast, and she's had serious relationships since then. Some people can forgive and move on. I think Marianne's done a better job of moving on since we separated than when we were together.

As you can see, I still made plenty of mistakes, but unlike the past, I repented them, corrected them or made sure I didn't repeat them. I was promoted to head of the leasing division at work. I taught the other loan officers how to handle leasing and medical finance. At that point, I was working long hours and pretty much running the company.

Amanda and I were married February 19, 2005. In August of that year, due to some lucky circumstances, I was able to purchase the company where I worked. On September 27, 2006, our daughter, Mikaila Olivia, was born. We visited my son after her birth, and at his request, brought his new little sister to his school for Show and Tell.

As thankful as I am that my life has turned out the way it has, I am one of a very few. Most of my friends were not as fortunate as I, and that continues to haunt me. I often think about the people I knew then, the people you've come to know in this book. It's difficult to remind myself that it's not my fault that I couldn't help them; I was as sick as they were.

Looking back

Today I want to be the best person I can be in all aspects of my life. Growing up, I wanted to be the best in the areas that people could see—the best at sports, the best looking, driving the best vehicle. There's a difference between being the best and being the best you can be. I always wished that I'd won the 800 meters in the state track meet. I wished that I hadn't injured my knee and ended my athletic career, but had I not gotten injured, my life would not be the way it is today. I am thankful for the experiences that got me to where I am now, and I regret all of the damage I caused.

CHAPTER FORTY
WHERE ARE THEY NOW?

The guys

Aaron, my friend from high school. He attends church and has a great family. Each of us felt that we should have been better examples to each other, and after I got out of boot camp, we made amends. We're now on the same soccer team.

James, my other high school friend. He's married and living in California with his wife and daughter and new born son. He and Aaron weren't around me when I got heavily into drugs, and I'm grateful for that.

Alex, my roommate at Portland State. He was one who was never going to deal drugs. The last I heard, he was selling ecstasy and had been robbed and beaten on several occasions.

Doug-E, the ringleader of the ecstasy/club scene. He graduated from Portland State, using drugs all of the time. Drinking was his enemy. He had a good job working for a bank, but ended up moving to California, where he's been kicked out of most of the clubs.

Eddie B., part of the ecstasy/speed group—the guy who always sang the blues about wanting to quit. He had a really nice girlfriend who pretty much supported him financially. He was one of the ones who mistakenly believed that he could leave his addiction behind if he changed his physical location. After several moves out of state, his girlfriend finally got sick of it and left him in Hawaii.

Brody, my first partner in dealing. In and out of jail for several years, he was serving time in southern Oregon the last I heard.

Jeremy, my brother. Married in Arizona with a baby on the way, he will graduate in 2007, when he will apply for dental school.

Craig, whose trademark was the drug residue around his nose. He served three years, one year of it in solitary for smacking an inmate with a chair for a remark about his girlfriend. After getting out, he was clean and had a good job at a welding company. He was spending time with Bobby J. and began using again, which led to identity theft and other criminal activity. In 2007, he was arrested and will probably serve up to ten years.

Joe, the insurance scammer who lived with Dee and me. Getting out of Portland at a good time for him, he went to Las Vegas, became a promoter and brought the rave scene to the area. If you look close enough, you might even spot his vanity plates around town—JOEKNOWS.

Mack, my co-worker from the Olive Garden. He was part of the group that followed Joe to Las Vegas. He's working for Joe now.

Artie, my right-hand man when I was manufacturing. When I saw him at my brother's wedding, I could see that he wasn't using. He has a job, has his life together and is now married.

Trey, who owned the stripper bar; son of Pinkie. The last I saw of him was when I was kidnapped. I haven't heard anything about him since, but I still think about him and wonder if he ever got his life together.

Joseph, the amber glass man with the California connection. He testified against his connection in California and served a few years in federal prison.

Derrick, the DJ who hosted many after-hours parties at his house. He's still spinning records, still using drugs. Most of his income is from what his girlfriend earns as a dancer.

DJ Jazz, the DJ who lived at the party pad with us. He moved to Las Vegas, where he was one of the top DJs. Now, he can't stay clean long enough even to get to a gig. Blacklisted in Vegas, he's now back in Portland, still using, and living in Derrick's basement.

The women

Karen, the first girl I lived with. She is still in touch with my sister, and we've e-mailed each other a few times. After we broke up, she realized that she didn't want any part of that lifestyle. She lives in California and has a successful career.

Faith, Joe's girlfriend. She and Joe broke up because of her drug use and dancing. She went full-steam ahead with both. Like Joe, she moved to Las Vegas, where she went to work as a dancer.

Holly, the stalker. She has a daughter now by one of the guys we used to hang out with. He had a crush on her for years, and once Holly gave up on me, they got together. She's still part of the group of users, and I can't imagine that her life is much different.

Ren, Brody's girlfriend, who stole drugs from me and tried to run me down in the van. She went to prison for two years, and from what I heard, she's managed to stay clean.

Dee, the stripper, my longtime girlfriend. The last time I saw her was the night she convinced a guy to put a gun to my head. After that, I heard that she was in jail for identity theft and forging checks. She briefly married a man who was always hitting on her when we were together. Her grandmother died, and I don't know what happened to Dee's children.

When I think about these people, I feel remorse, guilt and shame. They were my friends—some very good friends and others just drug friends—but I cared about each of them. Today they are my motivation and inspiration.

I learned from all of them. From Dee, I learned that we're products of our environment, and that it's difficult to change without any skills. From Pinkie, Trey's biker father, I learned that addicts rationalize their addictions by blaming an incident in their pasts. Pinkie used his guilt over killing a girl in Vietnam the same way I used my ADHD and my disappointment over my track injuries.

From Faith—who went from recreational drugs to a life of stripping and daily use—I saw how fast a person can fall in a matter of weeks. From Trey, I learned that an addict who is a friend is a conditional friend only. When it comes down to friendship or addiction, addiction wins every time.

DJ Jazz was one of the most talented DJs in the country. From him, I learned that talent doesn't matter if you can't manage your addiction. Without these people in my mind, I wouldn't have had the desire to change myself and to try to change the future for others.

When I first met Bobby J., I thought he was the coolest. Even in his addiction, he was a much more honest person than I was, and I wanted to be like him. The more I got to know him, the more I liked him. We painted together for years, and he lived with us at the party pad. Later, when I needed somewhere to stay, I could always crash at his place.

If you'd looked at the two of us back then, you'd bet that he and not I would be the one to straighten out his life. "Try to keep it under ninety," was his motto. He was the first one I ever knew who went to detox and rehab. His mother and sisters are recovering addicts. He's been around addiction and recovery long enough to know what you have to do to stay clean. Even with all of that knowledge, he's still not able to do it himself for more than short periods of time.

When I first got out of boot camp, he was still in jail. We didn't hang around together right away, although we talked on the phone. He was clean for almost a year when he called me and asked if he could come over and talk. It was six forty-five a.m. The only reason someone like him is up that early is when they've been up all night.

I had a feeling what he wanted to talk about, and I was right. He was out with a girl, he said. They'd been drinking and he ended up using meth, and once he started, he couldn't stop. What he wanted to talk about was that he'd ended up shooting meth, something not even I had done before—we'd always been against it.

He's been on and off since then. We had dinner in February 2007, and he told me that he and his girlfriend—who is also in recovery—got high for New Year's. Part of me wished that I could do that. I never wanted to miss out on the party, and that's still something I have to fight. I tried to tell him what he needed to do to stay clean, and that upset him because he felt I was preaching to him. There's nothing I can tell Bobby J. that he doesn't know about staying clean and following the program. He just needs to do it.

My hope is that with this book and my nonprofit I will be able to help if not my Bobby J., another Bobby J. or all of the younger Bobby J.s before there is a problem. Once there is a problem, it's a whole lot tougher to fix it.

800 Meters

If you had asked me at age sixteen the path I wanted to take in life, this wouldn't have been the one I would have chosen. I would never have put people down to make myself look better. I would never have taken that first drink. I would have never smoked a joint, snorted coke, dropped acid or used hash, mescaline, mushrooms, ecstasy, nitrous, GHB, Special K, heroin, crack or crystal meth. I wouldn't have engaged in premarital sex with multiple partners. I wouldn't have shot steroids. Instead, I would have stood up for what I believed from the start.

However, the sum of all of my decisions is who I am today. As much as I regret the losses and the people whose lives were affected by my choices, I believe that my decisions and experiences have put me in the position to help people in the same circumstances as I once was.

Looking forward

That life-changing experience I had in jail was the beginning of my commitment. I realized that if I had known how to deal with disappointment and failure, I may not have made such poor decisions. Life skills are much like conditioning in sports: effort expended before the race often determines the outcome. Preparation and training for the rigors of life can help prevent mistakes during the race, mistakes that can be costly to both the individual and society.

My nonprofit organization, A Generation Free, seeks to raise awareness for proactive life skills education in public schools. You can learn about our efforts by visiting our Website, www.agenerationfree.com. It is my hope that through proactive—not just reactive—education, we can build a stronger nation, one individual at a time.

APPENDIX
MY CRIMINAL RECORD

```
RR.RAB.OR0SBI000.LUMAN,MIKAEL DAVI - OWN RECORD.SID/10173809.PUR/M
###########################################################
###########################################################
BEP00040000. Dec 09, 2006  07:45:23
REUR  0004  LEDS
RR.RAB.OR0SBI000.LUMAN,MIKAEL DAVI - OWN RECORD.SID/10173809.PUR/M

OREGON CCH RECORD FOR SID/OR10173809 AS OF 2006/12/09 AT 07:45
BECAUSE ADDITIONS OR DELETIONS MAY BE MADE AT ANY TIME,
A NEW COPY SHOULD BE REQUESTED WHEN NEEDED FOR SUBSEQUENT USE
IF FURTHER DETAIL IS DESIRED, COMMUNICATE DIRECTLY TO CONTRIBUTOR

* CONVICTED FELON *
* SINGLE-SOURCE OFFENDER-RECORDS MAY EXIST
  THAT ARE NOT INDEXED IN NCIC-III *
* SAMPLE ON FILE FOR DNA PROFILING *
* ACTION ITEM: IF SUBJECT IS ARRESTED,
SUBMIT 'STATE' FINGERPRINT CARD ONLY - 'FBI' CARD NOT NEEDED *
SID/OR10173809 FBI/102125RA6
NAM/LUMAN,MIKAEL DAVID   DOB/1974/06/12  SEX/M  RAC/W  POB/UT
  HGT/600  WGT/155  HAIR/BROWN  EYE/GREEN  FPC/07AATT010508AATTAA02
* ADDITIONAL IDENTIFIERS *
SMT/SC ABDOM/SC CHIN/SC L FGR/SC R KNEE
DOB/1977/04/15
SOC/543198010
AKA/LUMEN,MIKAEL DAVID/LUMAN,JEREMY JOSEPH


CUSTODY    2001/10/09-A  OR003035C-CORRECTIONS INTAKE CENTER
  NAME USED/LUMAN,MIKAEL DAVID
  01 ORS 164.395 ROBBERY 3RD DEG-WASHINGTON CO
  02 ORS 475.992 CONTROLLED SUBSTANCE OFFENSE-DELIVER/MANUF 2 CTS-COLUMBIA CO
  03 ORS 475.992 CONTROLLED SUBSTANCE OFFENSE-POSSESS-COLUMBIA CO
  04 ORS 162.065 PERJURY-WASHINGTON CO
  05 ORS 475.992 CONTROLLED SUBSTANCE OFFENSE-DELIVER/MANUF 2 CTS-WASHINGTON CO
  COURT
  01  COURT ORI NOT RECEIVED                     CONVICTED-FELONY
      ORS 164.395 ROBBERY 3RD DEG
      8M JAIL    DOCKET #/C001379CR
  02  COURT ORI NOT RECEIVED                     CONVICTED-FELONY
      ORS 475.992 CONTROLLED SUBSTANCE OFFENSE-DELIVER/MANUF 2 CTS CS
      23M JAIL    DOCKET #/001289
  03  COURT ORI NOT RECEIVED                     CONVICTED-FELONY
      ORS 475.992 CONTROLLED SUBSTANCE OFFENSE-POSSESS
      23M JAIL    DOCKET #/001289
      PROVISION/CC
  04  COURT ORI NOT RECEIVED                     CONVICTED-FELONY
      ORS 162.065 PERJURY
      18M JAIL    DOCKET #/C002839CR
      PROVISION/CC
  05  COURT ORI NOT RECEIVED                     CONVICTED-FELONY
      ORS 475.992 CONTROLLED SUBSTANCE OFFENSE-DELIVER/MANUF
      18M JAIL    DOCKET #/C011202CR
      PROVISION/CS
  06  COURT ORI NOT RECEIVED                     CONVICTED-FELONY
      ORS 475.992 CONTROLLED SUBSTANCE OFFENSE-DELIVER/MANUF
      26M JAIL    DOCKET #/C011202CR
      PROVISION/CS

ARREST #16 2001/10/09    OR0030000-S0 CLACKAMAS COUNTY      FPN/33206932
```

```
NAME USED/LUMAN,MIKAEL DAVID    OCA/01040180
01 ORS 137.545 PROBATION VIOLATION-CONT SUBST

ARREST #15 2001/08/08    OR0340000-SO WASHINGTON COUNTY    FPN/37459180
NAME USED/LUMAN,MIKAEL DAVID    LAN/0112430
01 ORS 475.992 CONTROLLED SUBSTANCE OFFENSE-MANUF METHAMPHETAMINES
02 ORS 475.992 CONTROLLED SUBSTANCE OFFENSE-DELIVER METHAMPHETAMINES
03 ORS 475.992 CONTROLLED SUBSTANCE OFFENSE-POSSESS METHAMPHETAMINES
04 ORS 475.992 CONTROLLED SUBSTANCE OFFENSE-POSSESS FELONY
05 ORS 144.350 PAROLE VIOLATION
06 ORS 162.205 FAIL TO APPEAR 1ST DEG-BURG I 2 CTS
07 ORS 164.057 THEFT 1ST DEG - AGGRAVATED
08 ORS 164.395 ROBBERY 3RD DEG
09 ORS 162.065 PERJURY
10 ORS 162.205 FAIL TO APPEAR 1ST DEG-2 CTS
COURT
01  COURT ORI NOT RECEIVED                              NO COMPLAINT FILED
    ORS 164.057 THEFT 1ST DEG - AGGRAVATED
02  COURT ORI NOT RECEIVED                              NO COMPLAINT FILED
    ORS 164.395 ROBBERY 3RD DEG
*03 2001/09/21 OR034035J-CIR CRT HILLSBORO              CONVICTED-FELONY
    ORS 162.205 FAIL TO APPEAR 1ST DEG
    $105-FINE    6M JAIL    DOCKET #/C001924CR
*04 2001/09/21 OR034035J-CIR CRT HILLSBORO              CONVICTED-FELONY
    ORS 162.065 PERJURY
    $105-FINE    18M JAIL    DOCKET #/C002839CR
*05 2001/09/21 OR034035J-CIR CRT HILLSBORO              CONVICTED-FELONY
    ORS 475.992 CONTROLLED SUBSTANCE OFFENSE-DELIVER/MANUFACT/METHAMPHETAMINE
    18M JAIL    DOCKET #/C011202CR
*06 2001/09/21 OR034035J-CIR CRT HILLSBORO              CONVICTED-FELONY
    ORS 475.992 CONTROLLED SUBSTANCE OFFENSE-DELIVER/MANUFACT/METHAMPHETAMINE
    $105-FINE    26M JAIL    DOCKET #/C011202CR
*07 2001/09/21 OR034035J-CIR CRT HILLSBORO              DISMISSED
    ORS 475.992 CONTROLLED SUBSTANCE OFFENSE-POSSESS/METHAMPHETAMINE/FELONY/2
    CTS
    DOCKET #/C011202CR

ARREST #14 2000/05/13    OR0340000-SO WASHINGTON COUNTY    FPN/37154054
NAME USED/LUMAN,JEREMY JOSEPH    LAN/00007380
01 ORS 164.057 THEFT 1ST DEG - AGGRAVATED
02 ORS 164.395 ROBBERY 3RD DEG
03 ORS 164.272 UNLAWFUL ENTRY INTO MTR VEH
COURT
01  COURT ORI NOT RECEIVED                              NO COMPLAINT FILED
    ORS 164.272 UNLAWFUL ENTRY INTO MTR VEH
*02 2001/09/21 OR034035J-CIR CRT HILLSBORO              DISMISSED
    ORS 164.057 THEFT 1ST DEG - AGGRAVATED-FELONY
    DOCKET #/C001379CR
*03 2001/09/21 OR034035J-CIR CRT HILLSBORO              CONVICTED-FELONY
    ORS 164.395 ROBBERY 3RD DEG
    $105-FINE    8M JAIL    DOCKET #/C001379CR

ARREST #13 1998/01/28    OR0030000-SO CLACKAMAS COUNTY    FPN/32631121
NAME USED/LUMAN,MIKAEL DAVID    OCA/98001291
01 ORS 137.550 PROBATION VIOLATION-CONT SUBST 2 CTS

ARREST #12 1997/11/05    OR0340000-SO WASHINGTON COUNTY    FPN/36633924
NAME USED/LUMAN,MIKAEL DAVID    LAN/97013431
01 ORS 137.550 PROBATION VIOLATION-THEFT I
02 ORS 164.225 BURGLARY 1ST DEG
```

```
COURT
  01 1997/12/19 OR034035J-CIR CRT HILLSBORO            CONVICTED
   ,.ORS 137.550 PROBATION VIOLATION-THEFT I
     6M JAIL    DOCKET #/C940747CR
     PROVISION/PROB REVOKED
  02 2001/09/21 OR034035J-CIR CRT HILLSBORO            DISMISSED
     ORS 164.225 BURGLARY 1ST DEG
     DOCKET #/C973055CR

ARREST #11 1997/01/15    OR0030000-SO CLACKAMAS COUNTY    FPN/24369077
  NAME USED/LUMAN,MIKAEL DAVID    OCA/9700787
  01 ORS 475.992 CONTROLLED SUBSTANCE OFFENSE

ARREST #10 1996/12/13    OR0340000-SO WASHINGTON COUNTY    FPN/22556768
  NAME USED/LUMAN,MIKAEL DAVID    LAN/96013591
  01 ORS 137.550 PROBATION VIOLATION-THEFT I
  COURT
  01 1996/12/13 OR034035J-CIR CRT HILLSBORO            CONVICTED
     ORS 137.550 PROBATION VIOLATION-THEFT I
     DOCKET #/C940747CR
     PROVISION/PROB CONT

ARREST #09 1996/11/18    OR0340000-SO WASHINGTON COUNTY    FPN/22393552
  NAME USED/LUMAN,MIKAEL DAVID    LAN/96012610
  01 ORS 137.550 PROBATION VIOLATION-THEFT I

ARREST #08 1996/04/30    OR0030000-SO CLACKAMAS COUNTY    FPN/24260221
  NAME USED/LUMAN,MIKAEL DAVID    OCA/9607490
  01 ORS 475.992 CONTROLLED SUBSTANCE OFFENSE-2 CTS
  COURT
 *01 1997/01/22 OR003075J-CIR CRT OREGON CITY          CONVICTED-FELONY
     ORS 475.992 CONTROLLED SUBSTANCE OFFENSE-DELIVER/MANUFACT
     $94-FINE    24M PROB    DOCKET #/CR9600721
     PROVISION/30 CUST UNITS
 *02 1997/01/15 OR003075J-CIR CRT OREGON CITY          DISMISSED
     ORS 475.992 CONTROLLED SUBSTANCE OFFENSE-POSSESS/FELONY
     DOCKET #/CR9600721

ARREST #07 1996/04/16-A OR0340000-SO WASHINGTON COUNTY    FPN/21793721
  NAME USED/LUMAN,MIKAEL DAVID    LAN/96004258
  01 ORS 137.550 PROBATION VIOLATION-THEFT I
  02 ORS 162.195 FAIL TO APPEAR 2ND DEG
  COURT
  01 1996/04/16 OR034035J-CIR CRT HILLSBORO            CONVICTED
     ORS 137.550 PROBATION VIOLATION
     DOCKET #/C940767CR
     PROVISION/UNKN JAIL TIME/PROB CONT

ARREST #06 1996/04/16    OR0340000-SO WASHINGTON COUNTY    FPN/21792751
  NAME USED/LUMAN,MIKAEL DAVID    LAN/96004258
  01 ORS 137.550 PROBATION VIOLATION-THEFT I
  COURT
  01 1996/04/16 OR034035J-CIR CRT HILLSBORO            CONVICTED
     ORS 137.550 PROBATION VIOLATION
     15D JAIL    DOCKET #/C940747CR

ARREST #05 1994/04/06    OR0340000-SO WASHINGTON COUNTY    FPN/18552623
  NAME USED/LUMAN,MIKAEL DAVID    LAN/94002918
  01 ORS 164.055 THEFT 1ST DEG
  COURT
```

```
*01 1994/07/11 OR034035J-CIR CRT HILLSBORO        DISMISSED
    ORS 164.055 THEFT 1ST DEG-FELONY
 .. DOCKET #/C940747CR
*02 1994/07/11 OR034035J-CIR CRT HILLSBORO        CONVICTED-FELONY
    ORS 164.055 THEFT 1ST DEG
    $4851-FINE   2Y PROB   DOCKET #/C940747CR
    PROVISION/90 CUST UNITS

ARREST #04 1993/09/23    OR0340000-S0 WASHINGTON COUNTY    FPN/17656920
    NAME USED/LUMAN,MIKAEL DAVID    LAN/937897
    01 ORS 164.354 CRIMINAL MISCHIEF 2ND DEG
    02 ORS 164.045 THEFT 2ND DEG
    COURT
    01 1993/12/10 OR034033J-DIS CRT HILLSBORO     DISMISSED
       ORS 164.354 CRIMINAL MISCHIEF 2ND DEG
       DOCKET #/D9306323M
    02 1993/12/10 OR034033J-DIS CRT HILLSBORO     DISMISSED
       ORS 164.045 THEFT 2ND DEG
       DOCKET #/D9306323M

ARREST #03 1993/02/05    OR0340000-S0 WASHINGTON COUNTY    FPN/15533170
    NAME USED/LUMEN,MIKAEL DAVID    LAN/93001023
    01 ORS 137.550 PROBATION VIOLATION-THEFT II
    COURT
    01 1993/02/10 OR034033J-DIS CRT HILLSBORO     CONVICTED
       ORS 137.550 PROBATION VIOLATION
       DOCKET #/D9205685M
       PROVISION/UNKN FINE

ARREST #02 1992/10/19    OR0340000-S0 WASHINGTON COUNTY    FPN/16768422
    NAME USED/LUMAN,MIKAEL DAVID    LAN/92008991
    01 ORS 164.225 BURGLARY 1ST DEG
    02 ORS 161.450 CRIMINAL CONSPIRACY-BURG I
    COURT
    *01 1992/11/24 OR034035J-CIR CRT HILLSBORO    DISMISSED
       ORS 161.450 CRIMINAL CONSPIRACY-BURG I/FELONY
       DOCKET #/C921608CR
    *02 1992/11/24 OR034035J-CIR CRT HILLSBORO    CONVICTED-FELONY
       ORS 164.225 BURGLARY 1ST DEG
       $1220-FINE   3Y PROB   DOCKET #/C921608CR
       PROVISION/180 CUST UNITS
    03 1992/10/27 OR034033J-DIS CRT HILLSBORO     DIS CRT CASE
    TERMINATED
       ORS 164.225 BURGLARY 1ST DEG
       DOCKET #/D9207615F
    04 1992/10/27 OR034033J-DIS CRT HILLSBORO     DIS CRT CASE
    TERMINATED
       ORS 161.450 CRIMINAL CONSPIRACY-BURG I
       DOCKET #/D9207615F

ARREST #01 1992/08/13    OR0340000-S0 WASHINGTON COUNTY    FPN/17344848
    NAME USED/LUMAN,MIKAEL DAVID    LAN/92007071
    01 ORS 164.045 THEFT 2ND DEG
    COURT
    01 1992/08/13 OR034033J-DIS CRT HILLSBORO     CONVICTED-MISDEMEANOR
       ORS 164.045 THEFT 2ND DEG
       $50-FINE   1Y PROB   DOCKET #/D9205685M

ENTERED 1992/08/26  LAST UPDATED 2001/12/04
```

OREGON STATE POLICE
IDENTIFICATION SERVICES SECTION
3772. PORTLAND ROAD NE
SALEM, OREGON 97301-0312
OR0SBI000   (503) 378-3070

THE USE OF THIS RECORD IS CONTROLLED BY STATE AND FEDERAL REGULATIONS.
IT IS PROVIDED FOR OFFICIAL USE ONLY AND MAY BE USED ONLY FOR THE
PURPOSE REQUESTED